A SEASON WITH
SOLOMON

DAILY DEVOTIONS
FROM THE BOOK OF PROVERBS

MASTER PRESS

an imprint of Morgan James Publishing

BILL POWELL

A SEASON WITH SOLOMON

ISBN 978-160037-641-2 (paperback)

Library of Congress Control Number: 2009929438

Published by:

an imprint of Morgan James Publishing
1225 Franklin Ave. Ste 325
Garden City, NY 11530-1693
Toll Free 800-485-4943
www.MorganJamesPublishing.com

In an effort to support local communities, raise awareness and funds, Morgan James Publishing donates one percent of all book sales for the life of each book to Habitat for Humanity.
Get involved today, visit
www.HelpHabitatForHumanity.org.

Preface

Some books focus on one overall topic and cover the subject in detail presenting a lot about a little. Other books present a little about a lot covering many subjects succinctly. Devotionals are part of the latter genre. *A Season with Solomon* fits into this category as does the Book of Proverbs itself.

Introduction

News had a way of spreading even in ancient times. Word was that the King of Israel possessed something quite unique – something worth making a long trip to check out. And so she packed up her retinue and started out north.

It wasn't the abundance of wealth or the finest clothes that drew this queen from the southwestern tip of the Middle East. Nor was it major military might nor the newest architectural designs. It wasn't remarkable power and status that inspired the lengthy journey. She'd seen all that before. The curious ruler didn't come to observe a large entourage of servants or a multitude of fine-bred horses (in an age before the internal combustion engine). All the great kings had those.

It started with stories told by gruff and cynical traders. If nothing else, these ancient businessmen were keen observers. Not easily impressed, they reported a certain matchlessness in the leader of Israel. He was the wisest person they'd ever heard.

Thus the Queen of Sheba came to spend a season with Solomon -- ready to question -- ready to listen – ready to learn. If you'd interviewed her on the trip home and wondered aloud if her lofty expectations had been met, she would have excitedly exclaimed: "the half was not told me!" (1 Kings 10:7)

We can still hear Solomon speaking today in the Book of Proverbs. We can even spend a "season" with him without leaving our house! Yet more to the point, we can still hear Jesus Christ, the true source of Solomon's wisdom, speaking in these verses. For "one greater than Solomon is here!" (Luke 11:31, NRS)

Searching for an example of the spiritual hunger all should exhibit, Jesus pointed to this very lady. Her keen curiosity and arduous journey for wisdom beckon us today – to make great sacrifices in seeking anew for Christ our Wisdom in this foolish age.

The Book of Proverbs makes great claims regarding the value and "pay-off" concerning godly wisdom. "So you will find favor and good success in the sight of God and man (3:4)." Instruction therein enables us to make progress in all the areas that count in life.

Through wisdom the Lord enhances our development as His disciplined followers with God-honoring values, attitudes, standards and actions. Through wisdom He also informs and directs our activities as children, as spouses, as parents, as workers, as we handle all sorts of practical matters, as friends, as community citizens, as worshippers, and much more. Thus the admonition: "Wisdom is better than jewels and all that you may desire cannot compare with her (8:11)."

With the current "seminar" slant to learning some might ask, "Why did the king of Israel not employ a simplistic `7-Steps to Wisdom' approach? Why did he not combine all the data concerning parenting and family into one section, all the sayings about finances into another chapter, etc.?" I don't claim to know the answer but I'll suggest one response. Perhaps we might have been left with a trite and shallow understanding both of God and the complexities of life.

Also, Proverbs teaches us that God's wisdom is learned gradually and in measured doses -- a little here and a little there -- some in this fashion and some in that. Thus, Solomon was a generalist and an incrementalist. "How to" books and seminars have their place but can only make a small contribution when it comes to the vast topic of learning God's wisdom. Some things just take years of digging with hard work and sustained focus. The Lord simply does not operate on our time schedule.

Finally, this point can be made. In pursuing Christ's wisdom the very process of seeking is necessary and not simply the end product. Learning from the Lord is just as much about a journey as a destination. Indeed,

Jesus, our Wisdom, enjoins both the searching after as well as the finding.

Bon voyage . . .

Brief Instructions:

- The General Commitment is to seek to increase in God's wisdom.

  In three (3) consecutive months you will read through the entire Book of Proverbs once each month.

- The Daily Commitment is Three-fold.

  (1) READ A CHAPTER IN PROVERBS EACH DAY. Each day, you should read the chapter that corresponds to that numerical day of the month – Chapter One on the 1st, Chapter Two on the 2nd; Chapter Fifteen on the 15th and so on.

  (2) READ THE DEVOTIONAL EACH DAY as well.

  (3) KEEP A JOURNAL. As you proceed you will compile a journal indicating those areas of wisdom that strike you as most applicable to your life, values, relationships and circumstances.

At the conclusion you will review journal entries and choose five areas to emphasize in making up ground regarding your own "wisdom deficit" – to take with you into the immediate future.

As we simultaneously seek to grow in wisdom and that Christ might grow in us, we especially ask: "that the God of our Lord Jesus Christ, the Father of glory, may give you a spirit of wisdom and of revelation in the knowledge of Him. (Ephesians 1:17)"

Matt Henry's "Bad" Day

Proverbs 1:33. "But whoever listens to me will dwell secure and will be at ease, without dread of disaster. (ESV)"

Matthew Henry. That's a pretty well known name from long ago. He authored one of the most widely used Bible commentaries of all time. In other words, he's got a lot to say that's worth a listen. But he also lived, struggled and worshipped in the very real world.

Once, riding through the beautiful English countryside between preaching appointments, Henry was confronted and robbed. As far as he knew his life was also in danger. Before we review Henry's surprising response to this alarming episode, consider how often we permit even minor difficulties to upset all sense of contentment and peace.

Thus a less than Christ-focused perspective may end up "robbing" us again and again. But that was not the case with Matthew Henry. Here's what he wrote in retrospect:
- "First, let me be thankful because I was never robbed before.
- "Second, because although they took my money, they didn't take my life.
- "Third, because although they took all I had, it was not much and I have more elsewhere.
- "Fourth, because it was I who was robbed and not I who did the robbing."

His God-focused perspective and especially the last phrase indicate a man attuned to Christ. MH had long before become practiced in yielding all to the Lord – "whoever listens to Me will dwell secure."

On the flip side, many who ignore God seldom handle the various ups and downs in life as well. Not being inwardly yielded to Jesus, they often demonstrate an inability to handle outward disorders or inconveniences.

They may yo-yo between fear, anger, frustration, a sense of being offended, over-assertiveness or discouragement.

In closing, consider Matthew Henry's own comments on this very verse: To the one yielded to God, "he shall dwell under the special protection of Heaven, so that nothing shall do him any real hurt. He shall have no disquieting apprehensions of danger; he shall not only be safe from evil, but quiet from the fear of it."

What outward circumstances, relationships or other dynamics typically put you over the edge? Will you view your response then as convincing evidence that you are not really "listening" to God and not adequately yielded to Christ? Will you exchange your attempts at control or fretting for a lasting trust in the Lord and His settled peace?

Wise and Secure Investments

Proverbs 2:4-5. "If you seek her as silver and search for her as for hidden treasures; then you will discern the fear of the LORD and discover the knowledge of God. (NAU)"

In retrospect, we'd all be wise investors. What if we could return to 1986? For $21-a-share you could buy the initial public offering of Microsoft stock. Within a few years you'd be on the same track as Bill Gates and Paul Allen.

Or maybe you'd choose 1901. Use part of your money (sell off a little of the Microsoft stock) to go back in history and buy a small knoll just south of Beaumont, Texas. Then you could employee the crew of Anthony Lucas, an Austrian-born mining engineer, to supervise drilling.

On January 10, 1901, these workers ran about 700 feet of pipe into a 1,000-foot hole. Suddenly, there was a deep rumbling and moments later a geyser of oil gushed 200 feet above the 60-foot-high derrick. The spouting oil blew the drill pipe right out of the hole. You would have had a front-row seat at the birth of the modern petroleum industry and you would have owned the seat.

They eventually called that east Texas knoll, Spindletop. At over 3 million gallons of oil per day, the Lucas well produced 1,600 times more than any previous successful drilling.

Instead, God directs our investment ventures towards a different knoll – to Calvary. Through His Son, God has released a constant flow of untold wealth that will never cease production in time and eternity. Consider:

- the precious blood of the Lamb (shed at the cross)
- the outpouring of the Holy Spirit of God (that flows as a result of the cross)

11

- the gathering and perfecting of the saints (derived from the cross)
- and the coming of His mighty kingdom (that consummates the work of the cross).

Those who invest their time, heart, faith and obedience in seeking Christ and who willingly search for Him as for a treasure beyond all worth, will discover the fear and knowledge of God. Those who search diligently will become a means in God's mighty hands of bringing true wealth to their own families and also to a spiritually impoverished world.

"But we preach Christ crucified . . . . God chose what is foolish in the world to shame the wise; God chose what is weak in the world to shame the strong; God chose what is low and despised in the world, things that are not, to reduce to nothing things that are, so that no one might boast in the presence of God. He is the source of your life in Christ Jesus, who became for us wisdom from God and righteousness and sanctification and redemption." (1 Corinthians 1:23, 27-30, NRS)

The Last Law of Learning

Proverbs 3:1. "My son, do not forget my teaching, but let your heart keep my commandments, for length of days and years of life and peace they will add to you. (ESV)"

I've lived in three homes in Newport News, four different places in Richmond and in four separate dorm rooms at the University of Richmond. I could take you to every one of these addresses without the use of any high tech GPS device.

I've stayed in Holiday Inns, in Courtyard Marriotts, in other motels and in a number of foreign hotels. In most, I've remained but one or two nights. And if asked I'd have a very difficult time directing you to the business address of those establishments and an impossible time showing you to my specific room.

In the one, daily repetition etched the memory deep in my mind. In the other, the experience was short-lived; the memory was fleeting and the impression slight.

Those who make God and His Word an occasional "vacation" stop or a place to "stay" for a day or two on some brief spiritual journey forget easily. But those who make the Lord and His Teaching "home" do not easily forget. Thus, the last law of learning is "repetition."

Which would you say characterizes your treatment of Scripture recently: (a) a daily and passionate experience or (b) an occasional and passing occurrence?

Pray in accordance with Psalm 119: "How sweet are your words to my taste, sweeter than honey to my mouth! Through your precepts I get understanding; therefore I hate every false way. Your word is a lamp to my feet and a light to my path. (vs. 103-105)"

Light Eclipsing Darkness

Proverbs 4:18. "The path of the righteous is like the light of dawn, which shines brighter and brighter until full day. (ESV)"

Each morning when we rise and begin what too frequently becomes a distracted day on earth, the gift of natural light is meant to draw our attention higher and to the greater reality. For morning by morning the gradual increase of light as the sun progresses towards its mid-day zenith signifies our own steady conformity to Christ.

First, in the midst of the deepest darkness Jesus surprisingly arises in our life: "for God, who commanded the light to shine out of darkness, has shined in our hearts, to give the light of the knowledge of the glory of God in the face of Jesus Christ." (2 Corinthians 4:6, KJV)

Next, the Lord reshapes our life around His dominating principle of godly light: "knowing the time, that it is already the hour for you to awaken from sleep; for now salvation is nearer to us than when we believed. The night is almost gone and the day is near. Therefore let us lay aside the deeds of darkness and put on the armor of light." (Romans 13:11-12, NAU)

As the Light overcomes the darkness, God's new mercies come more and more into clear and singular focus. Each day Jesus looks down upon His chosen ones and with gracious favor gladly pronounces the great high priestly benediction: "The LORD bless you and keep you. The LORD make His face shine upon you and be gracious to you. The LORD lift up His countenance upon you and give you peace." (Numbers 6:24-26, ESV)

Consider this incredible promise: "whoever follows Me will not walk in darkness, but will have the Light of Life." (John 8:12, ESV) "This is the message we have heard from him and proclaim to you, that God is light, and in him is no darkness at all. If we say we have fellowship with him while we walk in darkness, we lie and do not practice the truth. But if we walk in the light, as he is in the light, we have fellowship with one another, and the blood of Jesus his Son cleanses us from all sin." (1 John 1:5-7, ESV)

Is there then any area of soul where you must ask Jesus to eclipse any remaining pockets of darkness?

Before They Happen

Proverb 5:14. "I was almost in utter ruin in the midst of the assembly and congregation. (NAU)"

A little quiz: when's the best time to "confess our faults one to another"?

The answer: Before they happen! The best course is to start talking about strong temptations and wrong inclinations ASAP and before they take us beyond mere thinking to action.

To whom do we talk? Obviously to God but also to trusted friends, strong in Jesus Christ, to whom we can confide and who can help us to detect and deflect a bad course (here in Proverbs 5:14 that would be defined as sexual temptation).

It's not enough to be in close proximity with Christians if we're making ruinous choices behind everyone's back. Carrying one "face" in church and another "face" somewhere else squelches grace.

Read backward from this verse and you'll find someone that for some time has not been in close personal relationship with the Lord Jesus Christ. And hasn't been up front with Christians either.

This verse also indicates another responsibility and activity. We have an obligation to those who are in the condition described: "Brethren, if any person is overtaken in misconduct or sin of any sort, you who are spiritual – who are responsive to and controlled by the Spirit – should set him right and restore and reinstate him, without any sense of superiority and with all gentleness, keeping an attentive eye on yourself, lest you should be tempted." (Galatians 6:1, Amplified)

To wrap up: How many have tried to "save face" in the early and mere mental stages of handling a personal struggle only to discover this reality. Their attempt to keep things to themselves never quelled the power and attraction of the temptation?

This question remains: Do you need to tell someone about your present struggles and faults? Will you do it today?

A Life with Certainty

Proverbs 6:21-22. Regarding the keeping and obeying of God's Words . . . "Bind them on your heart always; tie them around your neck. When you walk, they will lead you; when you lie down, they will watch over you; and whe n you awake, they will talk with you. (ESV)"

Unfortunately it's not just Scripture that becomes our constant companion. Instead it might be anxiety that walks with us, leads us, hounds us to sleep at night and is whispering at us on the morrow. Fear can constantly rob us so that we have little remaining emotional resources.

For others it might be resentment that plays that role. Unforgiveness is a very taxing attendant. A life of bitterness leads people to bind, not scripture verses, but offenses to their heart and to wear the wrongs of others as some sort of morbid "choker".

Still others experience a similarly disturbing dynamic regarding depression, ambition, arrogance, jealousy, greed or discontentment. Lust has become all too present as an escort for many who find themselves chained to its side. Any besetting sin takes on aspects of seeming "omnipresence" while becoming an unwanted universal companion.

But that's not the case in this proverb! Wisdom at work brings about an enviable daily experience, so that Christ's disciples come to have a:

- Life of Certainty -- from being decisively lead by the Spirit
- Life of Serenity -- from being watched over by God
- Life of instruction -- from being taught by Christ

What determines the difference? The better outcome derives from a deep respect for God and His Word. So much so that an individual loves and obeys Jesus Christ. The Old Testament teacher, Ezra, was said to have set his heart to study the law in order to practice it. We're called to establish the same consistent habits: "I commend you to God and to the word of His grace which is able to build you up and to give you the inheritance among all those who are sanctified." (Acts 20:32, ESV)

A Practical Suggestion: get in the habit of taking around small note cards with verses to memorize. "Bind" those words to your heart over and over and see what God will bring about through His grace.

Protective Eye-wear

Proverbs 7:2. "Keep my teachings as the apple of your eye . (ESV)" (Deuteronomy 32:10; Psalm 17:8).

In God-designed natural instinct we automatically guard the eye pupil. When threatened our eyelids close quickly, our hands rise suddenly to shield our face and our head moves abruptly to protect our sight at practically any cost.

We'll sustain serious injury to other areas of the body in order to defend the sight. Vision is that crucial. We don't allow anyone or anything (contact lenses aside) to touch the "apple of the eye."

It's no secret that we live in an increasingly careless age. The only thing many guard with diligence is their own prerogative to live as they prefer. In these declining times even some movements that masquerade as "Christian" inextricably minimize the absolute necessity for holiness. Blinded by this world, they ignore the great exhortation: "Strive . . . for the holiness without which no one will see the Lord." (Hebrews 12:14, ESV)

We've got a choice:

To be one who carefully safeguards Jesus' teachings as "the apple of our eye" – "to look with the eyes but to look through the conscience"* *(Quote from Ravi Zacharias)*; or become like Samson. The "apple" of his eye became increasingly rotten at the core with lust, loose sexuality and presumptions on grace. Later, his actual physical eyes were gouged out by enemies. Though Samson's strength was restored, his sight was not!

If we do the work to protect our spiritual vision up front, our spiritual sight will do the job of protecting us later on. "The eye is the lamp of the body," Jesus taught, "If therefore your eye is healthy, your whole body

21

will be full of light" (Matthew 6:22, ESV). What is the "lamp" of the body? This verse in Proverbs closes the circle. It's the place of the Lord's teachings (including the doing of them) in our life.

This question remains: which of Christ's teachings do you need to guard with an increased commitment and zeal? And additionally, what compromising objects are presently capturing the focus of your inner eye and must be surrendered to Jesus ?

Greater than > and Less than <

Proverbs 8:11. "For wisdom is better than jewels; and all desirable things cannot compare with her. (NAU)"

In this cynical age many would question whether any <u>one</u> thing can be viewed as incomparably valuable. It is through God's wisdom that we recognize the unsurpassed worth of Jesus Christ and thereby comprehend the comparative value of everything else.

In Christ's presence on earth significant reevaluation took place. After just one encounter with Jesus, Zacchaeus gave away over half his assets to the poor. Mary anointed the Lord in grateful worship with an extremely costly perfume (which might have been her super-expensive dowry). In a moment Nathanael and Saul of Tarsus changed fundamental and long-held beliefs about self, life, God, others and the future – and wholly embraced Jesus as the Messiah.

Scores more made a voluntary sacrifice of what was formerly most valuable. It all made perfect sense to them as the best way to express and solidify their depth of personal change; and to show that Jesus Christ indeed had no competition regarding their affections.

Wisdom first causes us to reassess the one who has been determining values. In other words we no longer trust ourselves but God. Crudely put, we learn we've been fired and Christ hired in our place. In the light of the Lord we begin reassessing all former values – to bring them into line with His instruction.

This discussion recalls phrases from Frances Havergal's great hymn and that affirm the incomparable nature and worth of Jesus. Consider Him in this light as you go through today:

Take my life, and let it be
Consecrated, Lord, to Thee;
Take my moments and my days,
Let them flow in ceaseless praise.

Take my silver and my gold:
Not a mite would I withhold;
Take my intellect, and use
Ev'ry pow'r as Thou shalt choose.

Take my will, and make it Thine,
It shall be no longer mine;
Take my heart, it is Thine own,
It shall be Thy royal throne.

Take my love, my Lord, I pour
At Thy feet its treasure store;
Take myself, and I will be,
Ever, only, all for Thee.

No Reserves, No Retreats, No Regrets

Proverbs 9:9. "Give instruction to a wise man and he will be still wiser. (ESV)"

Graduating from high school in 1905, his wealthy parents provided this young man with a trip around the world. In port after port the teen encountered a plethora of spiritual needs. "I'm going to give my life to prepare for the mission field," he wrote home. Upon his return some attempted to pour water on the plan. But the recent graduate responded by turning to the back of his Bible and carefully penning: NO RESERVES. That youth was William Borden, heir to the Borden Company family fortune.

Borden spent the next four years at Yale University and became an initiator in a profound campus awakening. "He came to college spiritually far ahead of any of us," a friend later stated. "He had already given his heart in full surrender to Christ. We who were his classmates learned to lean on him and find in him a strength that was solid as a rock."

Starting in September, Borden and three friends met each morning for prayer. By the conclusion of that freshman year some 150 students gathered weekly for intensive Bible study. During Borden's senior year over one thousand of Yale's students had become involved in weekly Christian events.

Outreach extended beyond campus. Borden and others assisted local widows, orphans and the disabled in nearby New Haven. They established the Yale Hope Mission and presented the gospel to the down and out. An observer wrote that Bill "might be found in the lower parts of the city at night, on the street, in a cheap lodging house or some restaurant to which he had taken a poor hungry fellow to feed him, seeking to lead men to Christ."

The missionary call was not forgotten. Borden was intrigued by the Muslim Kansu people-group of western China. Upon graduation from Yale (where he was president of Phi Beta Kappa in his senior year) Bill was approached with quite lucrative job offers. In response, Borden again turned to the end of his Bible and penned: NO RETREATS. He completed graduate school at Princeton Seminary and then excitedly sailed to Egypt to study Arabic. There he caught spinal meningitis and within a month the 25-year-old William Borden had died.

"When news of William Whiting Borden's death was cabled back to the U.S.," Mrs. Howard Taylor wrote, "the story was carried by nearly every American newspaper. A wave of sorrow went round the world. Borden not only gave away his wealth, but himself, in a way so joyous and natural that it seemed a privilege rather than a sacrifice."

When they found his Bible and turned to the back page, Borden had written a final phrase: NO REGRETS. "Give instruction to a wise man and he will be wiser still."

Resources:
"No Reserves. No Retreats. No Regrets."
(home.snu.edu/~HCULBERT/regret.htm)
Daily Bread, December 31, 1988
The Yale Standard, Fall 1970 edition
Mrs. Howard Taylor, *Borden of Yale '09: The Life that Counts* (Philadelphia: China Inland Mission)

The Hope that Bounces Back

Proverbs 10:28. "The hope of the righteous is gladness, but the expectation of the wicked perishes. (NAU)"

I once saw the coolest photograph of a tennis ball. The camera shutter had opened the exact moment when the ball was completely flattened against the strings of the racket. It looked anything but round and normal.

When we focus on just one moment, one event or even one season in life – things can look downright peculiar. At one point Job looked totally compressed. You cannot help but notice that Joseph endured a quick succession of depressing circumstances. Concentrating on the short-term alone, Hannah's desire to have a child seemed crushed.

All of us have moments when we feel just like that distorted tennis ball – mixed up, doubting and under enormous pressure. We may be left wondering and questioning: "What I want just isn't gonna happen. Where do I go from here? Why in the world is this taking place?"
Eventually, the Lord restored Job. God turned all that heart-crushing adversity into a much greater good for Joseph. Hannah waited, hoped, prayed and then had baby Samuel. On Saturday, the body of Jesus lay deathly still on a slab in the darkness. But early Sunday morning, God raised Him from the dead.

We shouldn't succumb to a "freeze frame" approach to life trying to fathom an unpleasant present. Wisdom calls us to observe more than the "flattened tennis ball" on the "circumstantial racket." In hope, we're to acknowledge that even in the midst of things we want to pass away the Lord still brings His gracious and good will to pass. "The hope of the righteous is gladness."

Some of you are in a "flattened" condition right now or you know someone who is. Take encouragement (and pass it along) from these great words:

"Hear me, O LORD, and be merciful to me! Help me, O LORD! You have turned my mourning into joyful dancing. You have taken away my garments of mourning and clothed me with joy that I might sing praises to you and not be silent. O LORD my God, I will give thanks to you forever!" (Psalm 30:11-12, NLT)

"Now may the God of peace who brought again from the dead our Lord Jesus, the great shepherd of the sheep, by the blood of the eternal covenant, equip you with everything good that you may do His will, working in us that which is pleasing in His sight, through Jesus Christ, to whom be glory forever and ever." (Hebrews 13:20-21, ESV)

Joining Pharisees Anonymous

Proverbs 11:12. "Whoever belittles his neighbor lacks sense, but a man of understanding remains silent. (ESV)"

During the early 1950's, Wisconsin Senator Joseph McCarthy recklessly accused hundreds of prominent Americans of being sympathetic to communism. McCarthy was eventually censured by the United States Senate. But before the administration of that corrective this mud-slinging politician had irresponsibly trashed dozens of reputations.

In 1952 during the height of the controversy, Democratic Congressman Mike Mansfield ran for the U.S. Senate-seat in Montana. Campaigning against Mansfield and on behalf of the Republican challenger, McCarthy derided the Democrat as a "Communist dupe."

Mansfield took the election and when he entered the Senate chamber for the first time McCarthy grabbed his arm. "Mike, how good to see you! How is everything in Montana these days?" Mansfield looked him in the eye and coolly replied, "Much better since you left, sir." He then turned and walked off. Belittling people has consequences. McCarthy had long before exhausted the good grace of many.

In truth, you can't "run" the good race for Jesus Christ while simultaneously "running" others down. "For in the way you judge, you will be judged, and by your standard of measure, it will be measured to you." (Matthew 7:2, NAU) A critical spirit "lacks" any legitimate spiritual standing and is not worthy of a hearing. "If anyone thinks he is religious and does not bridle his tongue but deceives his heart, this person's religion is worthless." (James 1:26, ESV)

We will all encounter real faults and flaws in others. What does the person of "understanding" do when that happens? He or she keeps quiet before people while interceding to the Heavenly Father on behalf of the less than perfect "neighbor." The very act of deriding others reveals a pronounced lack of godly judgment and the presence of a condemning judge.

Those truly seeking to please the Lord Jesus Christ shouldn't take the time to deride anyone else. They should be too busily engaged in distributing the mercy that they themselves needed and received through the love of God.

Consider this: when we believed on Jesus, He went ahead and took the initiative to enroll each of us in "Pharisees Anonymous." Have you sworn off a critical approach?

"Let no corrupting talk come out of your mouths, but only such as is good for building up, as fits the occasion, that it may give grace to those who hear. And do not grieve the Holy Spirit of God, by whom you were sealed for the day of redemption. Let all bitterness and wrath and anger and clamor and slander be put away from you, along with all malice. Be kind to one another, tenderhearted, forgiving one another, as God in Christ forgave you." (Ephesians 4:29-32, ESV)

Wisdom upends Self-Reliance

Proverbs 12:15. "The way of a fool is right in his own eyes, but a wise man listens to advice. (ESV)"

When it comes to "seeing" clearly, two good eyes are seldom sufficient.

It's "fool-like" to act as if our opinions, our plans, our beliefs and our convictions are right just because we "see" things that way. That's almost the same thing as concluding, "My perceptions are right because they're my perceptions!"

Misguided self-reliance can appear at every stage in life and ultimately to our detriment.

It's typical that young people want to prove themselves and assert their independence. So sometimes they don't seek or listen to advice on even the most consequential matters. They know their own mind and that's deemed sufficient. Through their immaturity some conclude that to rely on wise advice is the same thing as being controlled by others.

Middle-aged persons have the accumulation of life experience. These lessons afford them a great resource; yet not a comprehensive source. We should know better but the downward drag of self-reliance can afflict anyone at any time: "I'm an adult. I certainly know enough to make all these decisions without a need for additional input."

Young and old alike should consider this verse from Ecclesiastes: "Better was a poor and wise youth than an old and foolish king who no longer knew how to take advice." (4:13) The wise person who would seek the Lord and would properly cherish His will must of necessity become a practiced listener.

To "see" situations with extra sets of "eyes" doesn't threaten someone who possesses solid wisdom. It's no weakness to postpone deciding long enough to pursue a better informed decision. For listening to others doesn't commit use to following every offered piece of advice. Asking for another opinion is not tantamount to admitting weakness either.

The next occasion you have to make significant decisions will you become more committed to living out the latter part of this proverb?

An Accurate Predictor for our Future

Proverbs 13:20. "He that walks with wise men shall be wise, but the companion of fools will suffer harm. (NAU)"

While riding through city streets, I noticed an alcohol and drug treatment live-in home. The structure was located directly, and I mean directly, across the street from a Virginia ABC store. That struck me as beyond odd. Why would anyone locate a facility for recovering alcoholics less than 100 feet away from a store selling every sort of hard liquor?

Our relational proximity to godly or ungodly companions will also have its affects. That's the point under consideration today. But what of friends occupying the middle ground -- those who are not solidly wise and yet not classified as "fools"? Here's the catch. We tend to adopt the spiritual "temperature" of close friends. Some individuals can be as nice as they can be and we might share with them many of the same natural interests. But what if those pleasant companions are committed to nothing more than a tepid walk with Christ? And what if we desire developing a white-hot passion for the Lord Jesus Christ? Someone will change. Either we'll cool off and take on their lethargy or they will become more impassioned for God.

Make no mistake! Christians can and should be friendly with all sorts of people. Jesus made that plain: "As you wish that others would do to you, do so to them. If you love those who love you, what benefit is that to you? For even sinners love those who love them. And if you do good to those who do good to you, what benefit is that to you? For even sinners do the same . . . . But love your enemies, and do good, and lend, expecting nothing in return, and your reward will be great, and you will be sons of the Most High, for he is kind to the ungrateful and the evil. Be merciful, even as your Father is merciful." (Luke 6:31ff, ESV)

But we cannot make close friends of all. Choosing friends is one of the chief ways that we affirm soul priorities. That's especially true for teens. Want to know what's happening inside your child? Examine the close friendships. The choice for one set of companions over another group of companions is an accurate "compass" indicating heart direction.

Choosing friends that are pressing forward to know and serve the Lord has its good effect. "He that walks with wise men shall be wise." Christians can be friendly with many, indeed with all. But we cannot make close friends of all.

The Plimsoll Line

Proverbs 14:22. "Do they not go astray who devise evil? Those who devise good meet love and faithfulness. (ESV)"

In the 1800's they called them "coffin" ships. It's incredible to consider but some wealthy British merchants heavily insured unseaworthy and overloaded vessels. Then they set at home drinking tea while jeopardizing sailors' lives in sinking seas.

Mariners were required to sign a contract for a voyage and could be jailed if they did not remain on board when the ship set off – no matter how obviously and dangerously low in the water the vessel rode. Upon embarking some wrote touching letters to wives and children, to fathers and mothers, confessing their fears and saying their goodbyes. And more than a few never returned.

In 1868, Samuel Plimsoll was elected a Member of Parliament and made it his mission to put forward a bill to remedy this injustice. He suggested drawing a line on the hull of each boat doing business in British ports. Before a vessel departed an inspector would verify that the ship was properly loaded.

Plimsoll encountered stubborn resistance. The economy of Great Britain was dependent on shipping and the moneyed interests protested any "unreasonable" inspections and prophesied economic depression if the legislation was passed.

Plimsoll persevered. In 1872 to broadcast the need he published a book, *Our Seaman*. Popular support for the new measures swelled. In 1876, Parliament passed the Merchant Shipping Act requiring a mark on each vessel indicating safe load limits. Eventually, it became known and is still designated today as the Plimsoll line.

Wisdom does not make us disconnected and disinterested spiritual philosophers. It calls us to invest our time, talents, energies and passion under God's leading in real situations, in real needs and in real lives. We may not affect the enactment of national legislation but we are to love our neighbor as ourselves – to bear one another's burdens and so fulfill the law of Christ.

What good can you "devise" for another person today? Perhaps we can even be used of the Lord to "unload" some stress and weighty burdens. That initiative starts when we make the effort to notice those who are a little down today and "devise" some kindness for them.

Wise Words come from a Soft Heart

Proverbs 15:1. "A soft answer turns away wrath but a harsh word stirs up anger. (ESV)"

When does anger provoke a retaliatory response? Unfortunately, more times than not. Like an Australian boomerang though, it all has a way of coming right back at you.

The devil markets anger in the "double-edged" variety: it's destructive both to the object of wrath and to the one who is enraged. The "b" section of this proverb describes how unwise words only serve to escalate things to additional destructive levels. "Behold! How great a forest is set ablaze by a small fire!" (James 3:5, NRS)

How to end this unwise cycle? By becoming subject to the tender wisdom of Jesus Christ we will find that a "soft answer", the kind that quells rage, generally comes from a soft heart. In contrast, hard hearts only care about reacting. "You said this! So I'm justified in saying that! You did that! So I'll do this!" You find yourself corrupting the Golden Rule and doing unto others as they did unto you.

A tender heart replies differently both to Jesus and to people. Soft words emanate from those who refuse to place anger, or someone who is angry, in charge of their own response and character. There's a reverence for God and respect afforded even those who may not presently appear to deserve it.

How much more should we humble ourselves and offer "soft" words, when our actions or words are the cause of anger. That's almost surely what this verse addresses. We're coming into accord with God's wisdom:

- by affirming that we're wrong

- by not justifying ourselves

- by taking responsibility for change (in us, not the other!)

- by not using this event to set the "balance sheet" straight on all the previous offenses we've noted concerning the one we've just offended

- by plainly stating our fault and asking for forgiveness

- by not pressuring the other person to return us to his or her good graces immediately

- by walking "softly" (i.e., circumspectly) for a season afterward

- by [add your own additional items to the list].

'atarah tiph'arah

Proverbs 16:31. "A gray head is a crown of glory; [if] it is found in the way of righteousness. (NAU)"

GRAY HAIR!! It's an honor to have gray hair! What . . . !!!

How could it possibly be that the bane of American existence, the all-to-be-avoided appearance of age that brings many to the bottle (. . . the coloring bottle that is!) would be so positively designated.

Isn't this the real reason that those over forty suddenly <u>need</u> reading glasses? Because in fact they've been squinting once too often in the bathroom mirror and compromising their vision while plucking out those little offending "subjects". Have we in fact uncovered here a wide-spread conspiracy of less-than-biblical proportions between the sadly aging, those seemingly bland optometrists, the youthful hair care consortium and AARP?

Actually in a way this proverb is saying that gray hair is "kosher" hair; if it's been prepared in the right way that is. If accompanied with a life in-sync with righteousness, increasingly in-tune with the will of God and in harmony over a long period with the Lord. This concert of human aging with the Ancient of Days is termed in Hebrew, 'atarah tiph'arah, a crown of glory.

Finally, the verse is not about "whether you color or not," but whether those gray hairs (or dyed hairs) stand symbolically for innumerable days spent seeking to love Jesus Christ and His righteousness.

When God turns up the heat

Proverbs 17:3. "The refining pot is for silver and the furnace for gold, but the LORD tests hearts. (NAU)"

In our "wisdom" we sometimes fight the hands that place us in that "refining pot."

Life was going along just fine and then some event, circumstance, disappointment, or trial, some relational tension, decision, sin or a combination of the above brought us right to the lip. Now we're in. And we want out. ASAP appears typed in 20 font letters at the bottom of most of our prayers.

Any thought of being placed in the vicinity of a figurative "furnace" sounds daunting. In such situations our "wisdom" is short-sighted and often long-winded. We seek to avoid the very means God has providentially ordained for the present development and permanent improvement of our character and faith.

If we were more trusting or more dedicated to the removal of impurities we would respond differently. And perhaps we would be different sooner.

The Colonial Williamsburg Foundation employs a silversmith. This skilled artisan dresses in colonial garb and crafts items in a shop open to tourists. He sometimes stops to dialogue with visitors. "How do you know when the impurities are sufficiently removed during heating," one woman asked? The craftsman replied: "When I look into the crucible and can see my own image reflected clearly in the silver. Then I know it's pure and ready to use."

In His supreme moment of testing in the Garden of Gethsemane, when He faced the passion culminating at the cross, the Lord Jesus Christ prayed: "My Father, if it be possible, let this cup pass from me. Nevertheless, not as I will, but as you will. (Matthew 26:39, ESV)" His wisdom was far-sighted and short-winded – trusting all to God's care.

When Jesus "tries" your heart, what will your response be? Remember and take courage. For throughout the process you are not alone: "For Thou art with me, Thy rod and Thy staff they comfort me. (Psalm 23:4 , KJV)"

Hearing Both Sides

Proverbs 18:17. "The first to plead his case seems right, until another comes and questions him. (NAU)"

A while back I attended a traffic court session in which a friend had a case. That day, a well-dressed lady in her 60's was called forward for a traffic violation. The judge asked the police officer to relate her offense. She'd been speeding . . . going 63 in a 45 zone. Then the judge asked the lady what she had to say.

The woman seemed like everyone's favorite grandmother. She was respectful, gentle and soft-spoken. She could have doubled for a senior version of June Cleaver. Mrs. "Classy" told the judge that she was rushing a bit that day in order to get to her grandchild's school pageant, that she knew she was wrong and that she was sorry to take up the judge's valuable time.

Everyone in the courtroom, including the judge and the policeman, were plainly embarrassed even to be dealing with such an obviously wonderful citizen and grandmother. As a mere formality the judge turned to the prosecutor and asked about the previous driving record.

Then came the surprise! Reading the computer printout the lady prosecutor indicated that our favorite grandmother had many speeding tickets – in fact was close to being a habitual offender! Gasp! Everyone was shocked. The judge fumbled around for a moment for something to say and finally imposed a substantial fine and took her license for a time.

In heated disputes it's wise to delay formulating a strong opinion or expressing substantial advice until we've had the chance to listen to both viewpoints. Our perceptions and knowledge are always limited and often biased. We need input in order to give input. In practically every scenario both sides have at least contributed something to the problem. Thus it's likely that Christ has substantial lessons, even corrections, for both parties involved.

And what about occasions when we're the one seeking outside support in a disagreement or conflict? It's simply wrong to insist or demand that someone take our side without hearing the other side. The more emotional the situation the more we should encourage a third party to be unbiased. A warning claxon should sound if we ever object to another's desire to be objective.

What's actually most important to us? To get to the truth and learn wisdom from Jesus or to win and preserve our ease and ego?

"Lending" Money to God

Proverbs 19:17. "Whoever is generous to the poor lends to the LORD, and He will repay him for his deed. (ESV)"

The thought of making a "loan" to Jesus Christ presents some interesting scenarios, does it not?

How about a credit check? I don't think so! Need to get detailed information on how the money will be used? Not necessary! What sort of collateral does Christ have to offer? I'm not going to ask that question either! Would you broach the topic of pay-back to the Lord? Maybe set up a repayment schedule? And who's going to say, "Jesus, would you sign your name on this contract?"

How would you have handled the "donkey incident" in Jerusalem, Passover, 30 A.D. Some avid disciples (on Christ's personal instructions) showed up outside a house, unloosed an animal and began to walk off. Perhaps at that point the curious owner asked what was going on. We know the reply: "The Lord has need of it." (Mark 11:3, ESV)

"OK, sure, no problem." No doubt we'd look upon such a "loan" to Jesus as a gift. "Take it! Use it! I'm blessed to be helpful. I'm just happy to be involved, to be participating in what He's doing!"

This "lending" to the Lord is quite significant. And it's certainly NOT optional. Jesus strongly stated: "Then the righteous will answer him saying, 'Lord, when did we see you hungry and feed you, or thirsty and give you drink? And when did we see you a stranger and welcome you or naked and clothe you? And when did we see you sick or in prison and visit you?'"

"And the King will answer them, `Truly I say to you, as you did it to one of the least of these my brothers, you did it to me.'" (Matthew 25:37-40, ESV)

Godly wisdom inculcates a giving spirit, especially in providing for those who have the greatest need and the least ability to give back. Despite our tendencies, we're not to become insulated from the pain, difficulty or need of others and especially fellow Christians. Typically, the church has put 99.9% of its emphasis on tithing. Yet the Bible also stresses the importance of "contributing to the needs of saints." (Romans 12:13, NAU)

This week will you go out of your way and provide something for someone with a legitimate need, perhaps a single parent, in your church or at work?

The Saga of Azariah

Proverbs 20:10. "Unequal weights and unequal measures are both alike an abomination to the LORD. (ESV)"

SCENE: 975 B.C. Jerusalem. The Market. Camera pans in on Azariah the Trader. He's about 55 (old for the time). He wears a turban and has a calculating, wrinkled face.

Stop camera and focus on the trading table. Slowly pan across the variety of polished stone weights scattered about.

Then cut to Azariah haggling with some shoppers in the market. Display what the wiser citizens have long suspected. Azariah is a good (or should that be a bad) cheat. He's got standard weights. The problem is that he doesn't always use them.

On camera catch this: with practiced slight of hand and in the midst of a transaction the gruff old trader sometimes makes the switch from the proper weighted stone. When Azariah buys goods he sometimes uses the lighter weight to avoid paying full value. When he sells, it's the heavier stone so others will pay him more.

Next Scene and Camera Shot. There's a bit of a ruckus over one deal. It seems that widow Rachel has been swindled one too many times. Her adult sons, Amminadab and Assir, approach the table. They look angry. They look pretty strong too. We hear 'em demanding an adjustment or they're going to do some adjusting on Azariah's face. "We've had enough you old cheat," they're yelling.

Azariah usually pays a strong man to hang out and handle these confrontations. But he's not in the picture today. So Azariah pays a bit of money to the sons and says he can't understand what happened. He denies any deliberate deception.

Last Scene and Camera Shot. Show Azariah hastily packing up his goods, his money and his weights. The Big Two are still yelling at him. As Azariah leaves they pick up some weightier stones he's dropped and throw them at him. One hits his money bag and coins tumble out . . . as he exits the torn sack trails more money. The swindled traders and jilted shoppers pick up the loose coins. Close Scene.

This proverb has to do with more than business integrity. We are to consider how we judge and "weigh" things in our favor. When it comes to our clear mistake, it's easy to see ourselves as the prime candidate for mercy, patience, kindness, forgiveness, etc. But when it comes to the clear mistake of someone else we tend to see that person as a prime candidate to be ridden out of town "on a rail." How disconcerting to discover that our middle name is . . . "Azariah"!

Matthew 7:2-5: "For in the way you judge, you will be judged; and by your standard of measure, it will be measured to you. Why do you look at the speck that is in your brother's eye, but do not notice the log that is in your own eye? Or how can you say to your brother, 'Let me take the speck out of your eye,' and behold, the log is in your own eye? You hypocrite, first take the log out of your own eye, and then you will see clearly to take the speck out of your brother's eye.' (NAU)"

What about our Self-image?

Proverbs 21:2. "Every way of a man is right in his own eyes: but the Lord ponders the heart. (ESV)"

Jesus Christ is the <u>only</u> One in the universe who has the ultimate authority to say who we are and how we're doing. Does God's assessment of you mean more, infinitely more, than the good opinion of others or of even your own thinking?

Building our esteem on all the wrong things we become like the great image Daniel saw with the head of gold, arms of silver, a torso of bronze, legs or iron and feet of iron and clay. A stone not made by human hands suddenly struck the statue and the whole thing crumbled to dust. (Daniel 2:34-35) All esteem outside of Christ is destined for the same end.

High self-esteem is not a worthy goal but rather to have the esteem of the Most High God. Even Job, the godliest man on earth at that time, aggressively defended his own perceived goodness for the better part of 39 chapters. He sparred with his three friends in the attempt to bring them around to his sure opinion of himself. Encountering the unsearchable greatness of God sparked a change in Job. "Man is never sufficiently touched and affected by the awareness of his lowly state," John Calvin concluded, "until he has compared himself with God's majesty." (Institutes, 1, 1, 3).

Jesus said, "You are those who justify yourselves before men, but God knows your hearts. For what is exalted among men is an abomination in the sight of God." (Luke 16:15, ESV) With these brief words the apostle Paul clarifies things: "But with me it is a very small thing that I should be judged by you, or of man's judgment: yes, I judge not mine own self . . . . but he that judges me is the Lord." (1 Corinthians 4:3-4, KJV)

Here's the good news. When we abandon every self-authored basis of esteem and turn to Christ, then Jesus becomes our Divine Advocate. He gives us His righteousness and defends us with His very life -- ever interceding for our good. The Lord enables us to become increasingly oriented towards pleasing God.

Then this cluster of thoughts and goals, to be right in our own eyes, to be worthy in our own assessment, to gain the elevated esteem of others, becomes more and more an unfortunate relic of a deceived past. We start rejoicing that the "stone that struck the image became a great mountain and filled the whole earth." (Daniel 2:35, ESV) Our inner world is now filled with the elevated Christ rather than an exaggerated self.

Marked for Distinction

Proverbs 22:28. "Do not remove the ancient landmark that your ancestors set up. (NRS)"

Long before the days of GPS precision in surveying, boundary stones were used to define property lines. This side is mine. That side is my neighbor's. The essential landmark transcended memories and communicated across the generations.

When great-grandpa was gone, when the trees that marked the lines in his father's day were dead and used as firewood, when the fence posts that grandfather erected were rotted away, when father's memory was not what it once was, and when the son had become but a memory . . . the boundary rock remained.

We live in a time that discredits past times. This era tampers with "ancient boundary stones." One keen observer assessed recent changes in perception concerning the first day of the week: "Our great-grandfathers called it the Holy Sabbath. Our grandfathers called it the Sabbath. Our fathers called it Sunday. And we call it the weekend."

The same declining trend can be traced regarding marriage vows, sexual relationships and even unborn human life. The list goes on and on with reference to "boundaries" established by the Heavenly Father but tampered with by soiled and sinful human hands.

Jesus alone can restore the "ancient landmarks". We pray that He will!

Up to this point it may be easy to look down on the actions of others. So it's time to ask: how has Satan moved you and me to "remove the ancient boundary stone"? What markers are you ignoring or discarding? Name them before the Lord with a contrite heart.

We need more than the forgiveness of Christ here; we need Him to guide us in restoring the landmark to its rightful place. Is not the Holy Spirit, sent to teach and enable God's people, the expert regarding "ancient markers" and more precise than any GPS device?

Samuel Compton has well described our fault: "What you despise, you mark for extinction;" and the opposite remedy, "what you apprise, you mark for distinction."

The Good Kind of Payback

Proverbs 23:22. "Listen to your father who gave you life, and do not despise your mother when she is old. (ESV)"

Consider Jesus Christ on the cross writhing in the most intense agony in both body and soul! Without sleep for many hours, beaten bloody on his back and legs, sharp thorns pressing into the nerves on His head, nails piercing His hands and feet, fighting through pain for every breath to lift himself back up so that His lungs would fill with air. He was covered in blood, sweat and mocking spit. Jesus was suffering, going about the task of redemption.

In the midst of this excruciating scene, suddenly Jesus looked down and saw His grieving mother standing beside his remaining loyal follower, John. At that moment, Christ handed off the care of the woman who bore him to the beloved disciple: "'Woman, behold, your son!' Then He said to the disciple, 'Behold your mother!' And from that hour the disciple took her to his own home.'" (John 19:26-27, ESV)

Jesus expired. But while accomplishing the most important act in history and the salvation of the world of believers, the Lord was <u>thinking</u> about his mother's immediate comfort and long-term care!

So no matter what we're experiencing in life by way of difficulty or blessing, no matter what our career calling and its attending busyness, no matter what we're responsible for, we're to remain engaged with caring about and caring for parents in emotional and practical ways. They did it for us early. We do it for them late.

If your parents are no longer alive perhaps you can find some wonderful widow or widower to "adopt" in that capacity. There's plenty of need out there. Godly wisdom motivates us to make a difference whether in a face-to-face visit or on the phone, in writing or on line.

The Perseverance Wing

Proverbs 24:10. "If you faint in the day of adversity, your strength is small! (ESV)"

Just about anyone can exhibit strength in the best of times. Yet to remain strong in the worst of times reveals the substance of faith in Christ. When situations in life become less than appealing will we heed the appeal of perseverance?

Real endurance establishes character. Some are presently facing increasingly difficult circumstances or great relational stresses and perhaps ready to falter in the "day of adversity"! Draw near to Christ, the Great Sustainer: "He gives power to the faint, and to him who has no might he increases strength. Even youths shall faint and be weary, and young men shall fall exhausted; but they who wait for the LORD shall renew their strength; they shall mount up with wings like eagles; they shall run and not be weary; they shall walk and not faint." (Isaiah 40:29-31, ESV)

Notice how many prominent exhortations in Scripture belong in the Perseverance Wing of the Hall of Faith: "Only hold fast what you have until I come. The one who conquers and who keeps my works until the end, to him I will give authority over the nations." (Revelation 2:25-26, ESV) "You will be hated by all for My Name's sake. But the one who endures to the end will be saved." (Matthew 10:22, ESV) "I have fought the good fight, I have finished the race, I have kept the faith." (2 Timothy 4:7, ESV)

In former times, demonstrating firmness to the end was deemed an essential Christian marker. More and more we're running into the expectation, even among believers, of immediate and sustained gratification. Today, what happens when a relationship, a friendship or a circumstance doesn't live up to expectations? People seem to be more prone to "send it to the Recycle Bin."

So much has become disposable! With this thinking, anything that taxes our time, brain or finances becomes a motivation for immediate relief. Value has become proportionate to ease. Call it entitlement, or the effect of entertainment or something else.

Yet in valuing Christ and in serving the Lord we'll find that nothing has changed. Perseverance is expected and even required. We are to remain faithful to the Lord and to what He has commanded. The full "payoff" for spiritual endurance may not come, and all of it certainly won't come, in this life. That's why great tales of perseverance make it to the Hall of Faith.

"Indeed we call blessed those who showed endurance. You have heard of the endurance of Job and you have seen the purpose of the Lord, how the Lord is compassionate and merciful." (James 5:11, NRS)

The Lasting Impression

Proverbs 25:28. "A man without self-control is like a city broken into and left without walls. (ESV)"

All other qualities may work together to make a good first impression. But when all is said and done only character engraves a lasting impression. Will your final imprint be the picture of a city sacked by the world, or a citadel of integrity for Christ?

What is the root deficiency described in this proverb? It appears to be character, or rather the absence of Christ-standing character.

Because this man has checked out regarding godly self-control there is nothing to check the "credentials" of the visitors to his soul. The eye gate is open to practically any visual experience, to any stimulus, to any material object, to any movie scene, to any graphical display, etc. The ear gate is open to any sort of language, to any opinion, to any music, etc. Personal experience runs amuck. The ridiculous sense of freedom from constraints is on the way to becoming nothing more than license. When character falls flat the soul is unprotected.

Nothing else in life can enhance character whereas character enhances everything else in life. Money, success, prestige, reputation, talents, gifts, education, personality, intellect and wit are what Americans typically set great store by. Like Joseph's siblings they seek to be freed from their "younger brother" conniving to sell him away for a pittance. But with God's greater working they will eventually come and bow down before virtue.

Are there any breaches in your "walls" that need attention today? Through the teaching of the Holy Spirit and God's Word will you recommit yourself to monitor all that seeks to enter your soul through the eye gate and ear gate?

"For the grace of God has appeared, bringing salvation for all people, training us to renounce ungodliness and worldly passions, and to live self-controlled, upright, and godly lives in the present age, waiting for our blessed hope, the appearing of the glory of our great God and Savior Jesus Christ, who gave himself for us to redeem us from all lawlessness and to purify for himself a people for his own possession who are zealous for good works." (Titus 2:11-14, ESV)

Taming the Flames

Proverbs 26:21. "As charcoal to hot embers and wood to fire, so is a quarrelsome man for kindling strife. (ESV)"

It was a cold winter's night. Most of the neighbors had taken down Christmas decorations and put the now dried trees out for city pick-up. One of my young buddies suggested that we burn the discarded Christmas trees to get warm and pass the time. It sounded like a great idea.

The project crystallized and about ten wilting evergreens were dragged in front of the Pitchford house. (Needless to say, Mr. and Mrs. P. weren't at home). Someone ran and got matches. One lone voice questioned the burning project but to no avail.

Young boys, about to get an education, stood together while the match was struck. The next moment there was a roaring sound and we might as well have had the Tunguska meteor strike the neighborhood. The flames leaped thirty feet in the air and still seemed to rise higher. Then there was the awful awareness that things were about to get even worse.

A shout, "It's going to burn the house down."

Then, "Someone get a hose!"

A few used the occasion as incentive to go home early. Unfortunately, Frankie and Johnny Pitchford were at home!

Then almost as quickly as the fire started it just quit. Those few moments however were sheer terror. The rest of the winter the Pitchford front yard looked like a realistic set for a combat movie.

Just like those dried out Christmas trees the "quarrelsome" person of this proverb has all the wrong kind of potential. It's combustible. When expressed with argumentative words people get burned. It creates a scene. The household may also be in danger. What remains after an episode of strife is a black and charred place in hearts. And actually there's a war in progress.

Change is needed. Change is possible in Christ. He can tame those flames. They surely won't die down on their own! You must come to Him and yield those responses. If you're at all given to angry argumentation take a look at this: "'You shall love your neighbor as yourself.' But if you bite and devour one another, watch out that you are not consumed by one another. But I say, walk by the Spirit, and you will not gratify the desires of the flesh." (Galatians 5:14-16, ESV)

"Give us this day our daily bread"

Proverbs 27:18. "Whoever tends a fig tree will eat its fruit and he who guards his master will be honored. (ESV)"

My friend's father had quite a story. In the 1930's he started working as an aeronautical engineer at what eventually became NASA. One day, the supervisor popped in and asked him to conduct an elderly gentleman around the facility. That visitor happened to be Orville Wright. The great aviation pioneer was shown examples of how the present generation had built upon his aeronautical principles. Though the young engineer worked with the Wright brothers' ground-breaking ideas every day, meeting Orville Wright was at an entirely different level and became a time for deference.

Even the simple act of eating should bring us to God and grateful thanks for the Lord's wisdom-at-work and Fatherly care. It's appropriately humbling to work hard and then turn around and give the ultimate credit for the results to the Lord – even to petition Him to make His design work in this instance. Otherwise, we're quite presumptuous.

Truth is, with Harris Teeter just around the block and Farm Fresh not much farther, we often miss the connection between God's design and a full shopping cart. In the face of such abundance it does not always seem necessary to make the following request or to express the dependence implied: "Give us this day our daily bread."

Enter this proverb reminding us that in connection with food we're to think in terms of God's design for "sowing and reaping." We don't live in a haphazard universe where things occur by an endless series of accidents: "time + the elements + chance = everything else." This blatantly atheistic viewpoint contradicts the presence of a vital reality - the existence of intelligent design in the creation and the intelligence to understand and utilize that design.

61

Even though some ignore the Designer, yet everyone must utilize His design. "He who tends the fig tree will eat its fruit." Someone has to do the planting, watering, caring and harvesting. All is sustained by the ability to produce food.

Actually, the diligent use of the design is designed to provide us with more than an abundance to eat. It's meant to demonstrate the reality and goodness of the Designer Himself. Sometimes wisdom gets very simple:

God is Great! God is Good!
Let us thank Him for our food.
For by His Hand we have been fed;
Thank you, Lord, for daily bread.

"Yet will I rejoice . . ."

Proverbs 28:12. "When righteous men do rejoice, there is great glory; but when the wicked rise, a man is hidden. (KJV)"

It was an absolutely beautiful afternoon and I was attending a Promise Keepers gathering at RFK Stadium. 55,000 men were present. On a typical day the sky around Washington is filled with all sorts of aircraft. It's not unusual to see the latest passenger jets as well as technologically advanced military planes. No one in that large gathering paid them a second thought.

Suddenly a small bi-plane appeared, the kind you see dragging advertisements out over the ocean at the beach. The old plane slowly circled around the stadium perimeter. As more and more men looked heavenward you could hear cheering and clapping which built over the next half-minute to a full crescendo of sustained applause. Why this response for such a little antiquated craft? Trailing behind it was a big banner with these enlarged words, "Jesus is Lord."

Given, we're not often surrounded by 55,000 passionate worshippers. And we don't always live in the midst of encouraging circumstances. Yet no matter what, we can still join with those who down through the ages have worshipped in the manner described by Habakkuk:

"Though the fig tree should not blossom, nor fruit be on the vines, the produce of the olive fail and the fields yield no food, the flock be cut off from the fold and there be no herd in the stalls, yet I will rejoice in the LORD; I will take joy in the God of my salvation" (Habakkuk 3:17-18, ESV).

So it's not our use of the latest and greatest technology that establishes worship in our hearts. It's the resolve to acknowledge and proclaim His goodness and greatness in every circumstance that makes the difference.

"Rejoice in the Lord always and again I say rejoice." (Philippians 4:4, KJV)

The resultant "great glory" is never man-made or people-centered, merely focused on the worshippers or the style of worship. Rather, it's our recognition of our smallness to enunciate His Greatness that directs us and others heavenward.

The Mission is Submission

Proverbs 29:18. "Where there is no vision the people are unrestrained, but happy is he who keeps the law. (NAU)"

We live in the day of the "mission statement." We often hear this verse quoted as justification for developing a personal, family, church or corporate vision.

Mission statements and attending slogans summon the bottom-line purpose. It's a joy to read well-crafted summaries regarding solid Christian initiatives: "To Know Him and Make Him Known"; "Every Nation in Our Generation"; and "A Mind for Truth and a Heart for God". There are many others just as enlightening.

Yet we ought to be getting something else even more fundamental from this verse. In reality before the Lord's interested in our "mission" statement, He's going to check out our "submission" statement – the one we make with our life. The second half of this proverb "but happy is he who keeps the law," describes an obedience that reveals a heart characterized by submission.

In comparison it's relatively easy to come up with slang and slogan to present and market our church and organization. It's more of a challenge to conform our lives, goals, attitudes, motivations, thoughts, words and works, indeed to bring all the details of our life into the scrutiny of Christ. May God help us by His grace!

In the end, our legitimate mission comes from submission. No matter what we write down for ourselves the Word of God has anticipated us as disciples -- from what we pray to what we envision and embracing all our decision: "Your will be done on earth as it is in heaven . . . . for those whom He foreknew He also predestined to be conformed to the image of His Son, in order that He might be the first-born among many brethren . . . . make disciples of all nations . . . teaching them to observe all that

65

I commanded you . . . . that we may present everyone mature in Christ Jesus." (Matthew 6:10; Romans 8:29; Matthew 28:19-20; Colossians 1:28, ESV)

Most of us are initially more attracted to the thought of having an important mission than in coming into comprehensive submission. So we must be reminded over and over throughout our trek concerning Christ's great personal statement: "I always do the things that are pleasing" to the Father (John 8:29, ESV).

Wisdom Sometimes Makes us Self-Deprecating

Proverbs 30:2. "Surely I am too stupid to be a man. I have not the understanding of a man. (ESV)"

Arnold Palmer was not having his best day. And now, playing in the United States Open, he'd hit a shot right into a wide ditch. He walked around the golf ball a number of times contemplating options for recovery.

Then Arnie glanced up among the surrounding gallery and recognized Jim Murray, the Pulitzer Prize-winning sportswriter for the Los Angeles Times.

"Hey Jim," Palmer called out, "What would your hero, Ben Hogan, do in a situation like this?"

Murray eyed the man in trouble and slyly replied, "Well Arnie, Hogan wouldn't be in a situation like this."*

In this fragile age we're often told to think things that only inspire our confidence. We're told to be uniformly positive. We're told to concentrate on the bright side. We're told to avoid any sort of negatives. We're told triumphantalism will work.

Yet there's a time in every Christian's life when the most accurate insights will not take us in that direction at all. Proverbs records a real triumph in the personal awareness department right here, "Surely I am too stupid to be a man."

Have you had that thought or said something similar recently? It's probably a sign that you're quite sane and on the sure road to godly wisdom. In those humble moments our appreciation for Jesus Christ will not be diminished but rather enhanced by our encounter with a little reflection and self-knowledge.

"Christ Jesus came into the world to save sinners, of whom I am the foremost." (1 Timothy 1:15, ESV)   No, Jesus wouldn't be in a situation like this. But actually, He saves those who are.

Part of our calling on His wonderful Name is a besmirching of our own.

* Related by Rick Reilly.

NO Fear for the Future

Proverbs 31:21. [Descriptive of the Virtuous Woman] "She is not afraid of snow for her household, for all her household are clothed with scarlet. (ESV)"

Note how the ideal Hebrew wife approached the future with such confidence. How much more should the church, the bride of Christ, do the same! For has not Jesus walked on ahead? And for us, now is the time to follow Him with a steady trust over the crest of the hill on our long journey home!

From where does this blessed assurance originate? The good news is that Jesus has never gone anywhere except as a conqueror. When we follow and obey Christ, we're labeled as "more than conquerors". His faith, hope and love abide with us still. God's goodness and mercy bring up the rear and for each step of our excursion.

During this world's cold snaps, the church remains the continual object of Christ's constant love. Nothing is capable of separating us from His warming affection. The Heidelberg Catechism captures this God-ward conviction, asking: "What is your only comfort in life and in death?" The answer:

"That I, with body and soul, both in life and in death, am not my own but belong to my faithful Savior Jesus Christ who with His precious blood has fully satisfied for all my sins and redeemed me from all the power of the devil; and so preserves me that without the will of my Father in heaven not a hair can fall from my head.

"Indeed, that all things must work together for my salvation. Wherefore by His Holy Spirit, He also assures me of eternal life and makes me from the heart willing and ready from now on to live for Him."

What falls upon us as we travel through this often frigid world will never make us cold of heart. Are we not clothed as well and in garments washed in the blood of Jesus? He is more than what we need:

> Christ with me
> Christ before me
> Christ behind me
> Christ in me
> Christ beneath me
> Christ above me
> According to The Breastplate of St. Patrick

"Now may the God of peace who brought again from the dead our Lord Jesus, the great shepherd of the sheep, by the blood of the eternal covenant, equip you with everything good that you may do his will, working in us that which is pleasing in his sight, through Jesus Christ, to whom be glory forever and ever. Amen." (Hebrews 13:20-21, ESV)

"Old School"

Proverbs 1:1-5. "The proverbs of Solomon son of David, king of Israel: to know wisdom and instruction, to understand words of insight, to receive instruction in wise dealing, in righteousness, justice, and equity; to give prudence to the simple, knowledge and discretion to the youth - Let the wise hear and increase in learning, and the one who understands obtain guidance. (ESV)"

At the same time that our knowledge of the natural world has increased exponentially, we seem to be having a wisdom deficiency. The American establishment didn't gather together in some sinister board meeting late one night and decide: "Let's go secular!" But it happened anyway.

That general trend among adults affected the younger generations as well. Education was increasingly slanted toward facts while wisdom became passé. With the noted exceptions of racism and tolerance, nearly all instruction involving values was labeled "religious" and summarily dropped from the curriculum. That's ironic because the very decision to drop ethical instruction involves someone making some sort of <u>ethical</u> value-judgment as to what should and what should not be considered eligible for moral instruction.

In contrast to this present dominant tendency the Book of Proverbs places its highest priority on time-honored and God-respecting wisdom. The teaching from this unique Old Testament book covers more than the mere knowledge of physical facts and theorems. It provides what both young and old must have to succeed not just in a career, but in the myriad of life experiences, tasks and relationships.

Biblical wisdom educates us for God. It trains our hearts, not just our minds, to fulfill our responsibilities in time and eternity. It adds the lessons of faith without short-changing the practical living out of that faith in this world. Proverbs invites us to consider the great contrast between God's wise ways and our own tendencies and to undergo meaningful personal change.

There is one preeminent perception that the New Testament provides to complete our understanding of Proverbs. "But it is from Him that you have your life in Christ Jesus, whom God made our wisdom from God"! (1 Corinthians 1:30, AMP)

Let's join together then and ask the Lord Jesus for a "comeback" of the centrality of wisdom in our hearts, in our homes, in His church, in schools and in this declining world.

Our Shield in Everything, Not from Everything

Proverbs 2:7. "He stores up sound wisdom for the upright; He is a shield to those who walk in integrity. (ESV)"

The roof shields us from the elements -- from the sun, the rain and the snow. The overcoat shields us from the cold wind. Growing up I had an older friend who shielded me from a neighborhood bully. The U. S. Army shields us from those who would otherwise do us harm. And of course the ancient Jewish shields deflected the arrows and weapons of enemy combatants.

From what then does God shield us? The Lord is a shield for our faith that nothing will defeat it. Christ is a shield for our heart that nothing can turn it aside. God shields our mind that no thought can take precedence over His Word. Jesus shields us from the world and all its opinions and from the devil and all his minions.

Though God is Our Shield in all things, yet He does not shield us from everything. What has He promised to do? Jesus will protect us from the negative spiritual effect that particular circumstances might otherwise have upon us. As Romans 8:35, 37-39 boldly declares:

"Who will separate us from the love of Christ? Will tribulation, or distress, or persecution, or famine, or nakedness, or peril, or sword? . . . . But in all these things we overwhelmingly conquer through Him who loved us. For I am convinced that neither death, nor life, nor angels, nor principalities, nor things present, nor things to come, nor powers, nor height, nor depth, nor any other created thing, will be able to separate us from the love of God, which is in Christ Jesus our Lord. (NAU)"

The old cliché works here: it's one thing for the boat to be in the water and even surrounded by choppy seas. It's quite another thing for the water to

73

be in the boat. As Romans 8 conveys, the Lord brings us into numerous great waters but will not permit those dangers to sink us. "Many are the afflictions of the righteous," David declares, "but the Lord delivers him out of them all." (Psalm 34:19, ESV)

Ask yourself where your defenses are weak at present; and when you are most vulnerable. Is it when you are alone, or in a family situation, or at work, or perhaps at church? With integrity, bring each spotlighted weakness before the Lord and ask Him to become your soul's impenetrable shield.

The Strongest Kind of Affirmation

Proverbs 3:11-12. "My son, do not reject the discipline of the Lord or loathe His reproof, for whom the Lord loves He reproves, even as a father corrects the son in whom he delights. (NAU)"

Whether it makes sense to us or not, divine discipline is the strongest kind of affirmation. The Lord is always looking out for our long-term interest. And when we need to be redirected God will sacrifice the short-term for a better long-term <u>every</u> time.

Correction, which we so frequently view in negative terms, has the most encouraging results when God is its Author:

"Now, discipline always seems painful rather than pleasant at the time, but later it yields the peaceful fruit of righteousness to those who have been trained by it. Therefore lift your drooping hands and strengthen your weak knees and make straight paths for your feet, so that what is lame may not be put out of joint, but rather be healed." (Hebrews 12:11-13, NRS)

In contrast we're typically short-sighted. We'd rather be made to feel better in the moment than be made better in the end. We become quickly "wearied" under the Lord's rod. There are numerous reasons why, if it were left up to us, that we would avoid discipline:

- because typically we see it as losing face
- because we're not always on board with our wrongs being exposed
- because we don't like for the easy "flow" and light-heartedness of life to be disturbed
- because we are not solidly convinced that change and adjustment are necessary or even possible

No matter our take on things, the "discipline of the Lord" is a normal and repeated part of being a Christian. Christ does not ask for our permission or wait on our willing cooperation concerning correction. This exhortation assumes that discipline will happen. Our response to that chastening is the issue.

Will you hold up your spirit in trust to Jesus and not become hardened or discouraged when God employs His remedy? It certainly pleases the Lord when He sees us demonstrate patient trust and conduct ourselves with faith in His wise administering of a corrective session or season.

A Spiritual Vigilance

Proverbs 4:23. "Keep your heart with all diligence, for out of it spring the issues of life. (NKJ)"

Many nights during the infamous Blitz of 1940, mothers gathered on London rooftops. And they weren't sipping tea.

Devoted to the well-being of their children these erstwhile ladies became practiced at discerning one noise. When the terrifying whine of Nazi bombs came too close for comfort the mothers leaped down the stairs to their flats. They had little time to pick up babies and small children and dash for the basement for the best protection they could afford.

In all sorts of weather, on good days and bad days, when tired and exhausted, when sleepy, through it all the mothers marched together to the rooftop. They remain a picture of vigilance today.

Proverbs 4 calls us to a different sort of task – a vigilance of soul. Our present war is not as obvious as bombs dropping on our neighborhood. But a foe more wicked than Adolph Hitler assaults us regularly.

Satan's objective is to keep the heart from Jesus Christ. Short of that his objective is to turn the heart away from the Lord and toward ready substitutes. Short of that his objective is to weigh the heart down with excessive burdens and fears.

This proverb literally says, "Keep your heart with all keepings." The redundancy is for emphasis! Those who would follow Christ must resist the enemy time after time. The apostle Peter wrote: "Be sober-minded; be watchful. Your adversary the devil prowls around like a roaring lion, seeking someone to devour. Resist him, firm in your faith." (1 Peter 5:8-9,ESV) When those beguiling thoughts or base temptations erupt we have this holy charge: "Submit therefore to God. Resist the devil and he will flee from you." (James 4:7, NAU)

Once again, our great hope derives from the Lord Jesus. On our behalf Christ made this request: "Holy Father, protect them in Your Name" (John 17:11, NRS). And so we also pray, "Our Father who is in heaven, deliver us from evil."

May these words of John have their full force regarding every saint: "I write to you, young men, because you are strong, and the word of God abides in you, and you have overcome the evil one." (1 John 2:14, ESV)

Mt. Rushmore Marriages

Proverbs 5:18. "Rejoice in the wife of your youth . . . (ESV)"

Just happy to be together . . .   My parents met on a blind date in January 1942. They married in July of that year. My father was 27 and my mother was 20. They celebrated sixty-four anniversaries together.

When my dad was 91, he could hardly get around at all and suffered from degrees of dementia. But I still saw him greet my mom with a tender kiss – still happy to be together. During this long run they certainly had their share of things to be in conflict over but nothing ever eroded their mutual care. They had a Mt. Rushmore marriage.

I was privileged to see in their lives this verse fulfilled. Their joyful relationship is a great asset. It's been one of the "silent" classes in life. There was no official teacher, no official classroom, no official lectures, no official tests and no official grades, but with an abundance of great lessons.

Age changes many things, physical and otherwise. On the other hand, wisdom tells us what to keep the same. This exhortation to husbands is one of those: "Rejoice with the wife of your youth." Just happy to be together . . . that should never change.

Those who fulfill this proverb best picture the love of Jesus Christ for His bride, prevailing in the moment and persevering to the end.

Transforming "Prodigal" Feet

Proverbs 6:16-18. **"There are six things which the LORD hates, yes, seven which are an abomination to Him . . . feet that run rapidly to evil.** (NAU) "

We had prodigal feet. When exposed to The Light we scurried for the darkness like a suddenly discovered cockroach. As Adam's descendants we ran towards the wrong and away from the Lord.

Yes, God hates "feet that run rapidly to evil." But He certainly loves to empower steps that bring us back to Him. It takes a transforming miracle of God for that transition to happen. Through Jesus Christ our "feet" can be newly made to "stand firm" in the Lord; to "walk in the Spirit;" and to "run with patience" the race set before us! (Ephesians 6:14; Galatians 5:16; Hebrews 12:1, NAU)

What will produce these wonderful changes? The "feet" of Jesus Himself! First the Son of God became a man and walked in perfect step with the Father. We can say that Jesus had Obedient Feet – ours strayed but His stayed.

One day the Son of God surrendered those same feet to the jagged spike at the cross. His Bleeding Feet paid the cost for all of our transgressions so that we, like the prodigal son, might return step by step to the Heavenly Father and the abundance of the heavenly home.

Is it any wonder then that Mary took hold of His feet in worship, anointing them with costly perfume and with tears of gratitude for His compassionate forgiveness? Should we be surprised that the beloved disciple John, seeing the Lord glorified in heaven, fell at His feet as "dead" in worship -- in recognition of His overwhelming greatness? (John 12:3; Revelation 1:17, ESV)

For God loves Redeemed Feet that run rapidly to Jesus Christ. And now we're called to carry this same Good News concerning Christ's death and resurrection even to those who are still "running" to evil: "How beautiful upon the mountains are the feet of him who bring good news, who publishes peace, who brings good news of happiness, who publishes salvation, who say to Zion, `Your God reigns!'" (Isaiah 52:7, ESV)

Locating the "Exit" Light

Proverbs 7:7-10. "And I saw among the naive, and discerned among the youths a young man lacking sense, passing through the street near her corner; and he takes the way to her house, in the twilight, in the evening, in the black and dark night. And behold, a woman comes to meet him, dressed as a harlot and cunning of heart. (NAU)"

This is Level One temptation. Note the ominous progression towards darkness and from a mere suggestion to a growing obsession. Sadly, this allegorical story does not end well. The decision by the young man to yield to lust will cost him "his life." It is a classic what-not-to-do tale and it is both practical and symbolic.

The temptress represents anything, whether sexual in nature or not, that would lure us away from the Lord and His wise ways. We are to read the allegory in a generally applicable manner. In the natural world, little grows in the dark. Yet spiritually, what contradicts Jesus Christ and the safety of His will thrives in the "black and dark night." At the inception of enticement the Children of the Light wisely resist those attractive pulls.

With the departure of the sun's last bending rays, the harlot suddenly immerges from the shadows. She becomes the tantalizing focus of this young man's willful bending from light to darkness. What he's taken hold of in pleasurable anticipation has in fact taken hold of him. What draws the young man initially, eventually detains him and finally defeats him.

Stop the story here. Return to reality and to your own life. Is there anything at present that attracts you toward the "twilight"? Are you stepping into the "evening" anywhere? or, God forbid, have you been sitting in "absolute darkness"?

If so, pray now that you may clearly hear great delivering voice of Jesus: "saying to those who are bound, 'Go forth,' and to those who are in darkness, 'Show yourselves.'" (Isaiah 49:9, NAU)   It is Christ's power that is unmatched and can bring you again to liberty and to a bright and hopeful place where you will have nothing to hide.

Wisdom teaches us to value Christ supremely and preeminently in matters involving a clear conscience. Jesus was tempted yet without succumbing. Temptation is not sin. And the Lord has promised on His integrity to help you: "No temptation has overtaken you that is not common to man. God is faithful, and he will not let you be tempted beyond your ability, but with the temptation he will also provide the way of escape, that you may be able to endure it." (1 Corinthians 10:13, ESV)

Durable Riches

Proverbs 8:18. "Riches and honor are with me: enduring wealth and righteousness. (NAU)"

Some years ago two global companies, Enron and Worldcom, "cooked" their books and subsequently "burned" their investors.

Profits and assets were deliberately and regularly inflated to make these companies appear financially super-prosperous (and what they were in fact was supercilious). Enron appropriately became known after its slanted logo as -- the "Crooked E."

Leaders of those corporate scams became rich at the expense of honor. Some were put on trial and jailed. Yet "a good name is rather to be chosen than great riches" (Proverbs 22:1, KJV) Many investors, who had thrown caution to the wind, reaped the whirlwind.

The Lesson? The world can make and market riches but not durable riches. Only God can do that. Day after day Wisdom is calling to us to invest our lives in becoming "rich toward God" and "rich in faith" (Proverbs 1; Luke 12:21; James 2:5, ESV).

Regarding stocks you may say, "I have little to invest! I don't have much disposable income." But the same can't be said regarding your reply to God. What He requires is that you take stock of your life and then turn it over to Him. Will you do that today?

All God's riches are subservient to His righteousness and His own high honor. It's Jesus' intention to make us wealthy in joy, in peace, in purpose, in hope, in faith, in love, in holiness, in wisdom, in kindness and in every enduring virtue. For He said, "I am come that they might have life and that they might have it more abundantly." (John 10:10, KJV)

Christ emptied Himself of the experience of heavenly riches in order to become a man. Jesus suffered dishonor at the cross – the righteous for the unrighteous. His humiliation became the means of our exaltation and the solitary path to honor. His deliberate poverty became the sole source of permanent riches for us.

Note this response to these most gracious acts: "Indeed, I count everything as loss because of the surpassing worth of knowing Christ Jesus my Lord. For his sake I have suffered the loss of all things and count them as rubbish, in order that I may gain Christ . . . . And my God will supply every need of yours according to His riches in glory in Christ Jesus." (Philippians 3:8; 4:19, ESV)

Jesus lost His life that you might gain yours. Jesus experienced dishonor to take away yours. Durable riches and righteous honor remain with Him and with those who draw near to God through Him.

The Responsibility of the Instructor

Proverbs 9:9. "Give instruction to a wise man and he will be still wiser; teach a righteous man and he will increase in learning. (ESV)"

We usually connect teaching with some academic setting. Yet biblical discipleship is typically more relational than scholastic. It entails more than passing on information. It's all about caring for someone else and educating the spirit as well as the mind.

This sort of instruction conveys the power to stand before God, to stand through God and to stand for God; to keep Christians on their feet in a world that's slipping away. How is this accomplished, especially with younger men and women?

Stand by them . . . when someone needs someone, be there. Maybe <u>speak</u> words of encouragement. Or maybe just be there in <u>silence</u>. The opportunity to pass along lessons and principles often follows after we make the personal choice to stand by someone in difficulty or a time of need. Recall the old adage: "People don't care what you know until they know how much you care."

Stand tall for them . . . let them see the Lord's character in you. Set them a high mark so that they can get high marks in Christ.

Stand before them . . . and give enunciation to wise insights in order that they can clearly hear the voice of Jesus through you: "Take my yoke on you and learn of me."

Stand up to them . . . on the hopefully rare occasion when that becomes necessary and so that the world, the flesh and the devil don't erode their faith and obedience. Model submission to Christ's rule so that they grasp Christ's message, "As many as I love, I rebuke and chasten, be zealous and repent."

Stand around with them . . . depending on the nature of your relationship (i.e., parent, mentor or friend), make them your companions as well. Don't always be an intense instructor or determined confronter. Remember that Jesus said to the disciples, "I call you my friends."

Stand behind them . . . when it's their time to stand out. Push them forward that they may take part in fulfilling His commission through their own call and gifting : "Disciple all nations. Teach them all that I've commanded you."

Finally, pray that those whom you influence may know that Jesus Christ:
- Stands at the door and knocks -- as Savior
- Stands over them – as Lord
- Stands by them -- as Advocate
- Stands with them -- as Friend
- Stands tall for them -- as Master
- Stands up to them -- as Discipler
- Stands before them -- as Teacher
- Stand behind them -- as Encourager
- Stands ready to return for them -- as Messiah!

The Balancing Act: Talking and Listening

Proverbs 10:19. "When there are many words, transgression is unavoidable. But he who restrains his lips is wise. (NAU)"

Before people listen to what we say they first take into consideration whether we're considerate.

Restaurant Scene. You notice two persons being seated two tables over. One begins talking when they sit down, continues talking through the entire meal and is still talking when you get up to leave.

That person never asks questions and never expresses interest in the other's opinions – never makes the effort to include the other in real dialogue. Any considerate interaction is drowned out by the constant onslaught of words. The dominating talker may as well be seated across from a gigantic ear.

At some point we've got to ask ourselves, "Why would anyone want to listen to a `multitude of words' from me?" The obvious answer is, they don't! Once we speak without any regard to whether others want to listen to us, we've crossed over some line. If we think we have that much knowledge or wisdom to impart, perhaps it's time to do a lot more listening. We can take the opportunity to draw others out rather than driving them out.

Assertive individuals presumptuously dominate conversations. Others seek to entertain themselves by talking. Some become so enamored by their own opinions and perceptions that they ignore the subtle hints of disinterest from the trapped and often frustrated listener.

And all this precedes the issue raised by the proverb, that the more we talk the more likely we are to say wrong things. Wisdom teaches us to be more judicious and to say less with better effect.

89

As a parent, or as a son or daughter, or as a friend, or as a co-worker, or as a participant in a small group, or in whatever role you find yourself, make the choice today to listen and thereby affirm and respect those around you. Ask others their take on things before you give your own.

You Can't Afford to Hoard

Proverbs 11:24-25. "One gives freely, yet grows all the richer; another withholds what he should give and only suffers want. Whoever brings blessing will be enriched and one who waters will himself be watered. (ESV)"

My friend had numerous envelopes before him on the dining room table. Each had a name inscribed by hand. I didn't know what my buddy was up to but he certainly looked like a "bookie" distributing the daily winnings. So I asked.

Each payday my generous friend set aside what he felt he could give to persons in need. He gave to the church by check. These envelopes were over and above that as he distributed "to the necessity of the saints." Over the years it has been amazing to see the way Christ has used this individual (usually anonymously) to bring practical help to single parents and children, to those going through a difficult season, to overseas missions, to those in ministry, and on and on. You couldn't be around a more refreshing person either.

The medical MRI provides accurate details for what's happening inside the body. The Book of Proverbs provides an "MRI" on the healthy soul. Here we learn that those who possess wisdom are unfailingly generous.

What's included in "giving"? It's certainly financial but it's also more than financial. Giving is about pitching in and helping on tasks and projects to relieve one person from having too much to carry or carry out. It's also time spent with others for all sorts of reasons. It's speaking encouraging words or providing a listening ear. It's being a silent presence of support or giving whatever else is required in the given situation. It's taking all we have and placing it at God's disposal.

Giving is an indicator of the future as well. Those who distribute "freely" with a right heart and those that share generously will receive from God and others in return. People will reciprocate. And when they don't, God will! And if not in this life, then surely in the next!

Jesus stated, "And whoever gives one of these little ones even a cup of cold water because he is a disciple, truly, I say to you, he will by no means lose his reward. (Matthew 10:42, ESV)"   "God is not so unjust as to overlook your work and the love that you showed for His sake in serving the saints, as you still do. Hebrews 6:10, ESV)" "For with the measure you use, it will be measured back to you. Luke 6:38, ESV)"

Generosity marks the godly. The stingy don't resemble God at all.

Today's Match: Anxiety versus Wisdom

Proverbs 12:25. "Anxiety weighs down the human heart, but a good word cheers it up. (NRS)"

Philip Melancthon was a compatriot with Martin Luther in the Protestant Reformation. Melancthon was a world-class Christian teacher but he was sometimes a world-class worrier as well. One afternoon Luther popped in to visit Melancthon who was evidently weighted down. He fidgeted and expressed an across-the-board anxiety about life. Perceiving his dear friend's struggle, Luther gently admonished: "May Philip cease to rule the world!"

Is God not able to govern our personal history? It cannot be otherwise! It is His plan to break the fear-cycle and habit. Christ encourages us in the face of every discouragement and is well able to lift all our anxieties: "These things I have spoken unto you, that in me you might have peace. In the world you shall have tribulation: but be of good cheer; I have overcome the world." (John 16:33, KJV)

The sooner we embrace God's sovereign care the sooner we may gladly declare: "for I know whom I have believed, and I am convinced that He is able to guard what I have entrusted to Him until that Day." (2 Timothy 1:12, NAU)

Yet for some, to grow in years is to grow in fears. Consider the analogy of physical exercise. Lifting weights properly strengthens muscles. But in regards to anxiety the opposite holds true. The more fear we lift the more weighed down and weaker in faith we become.

Christ alone is unerringly trustworthy. God would have us to experience the wonderful fruits of our faithful dependence upon Him: "You keep him in perfect peace whose mind is stayed on you, because he trusts in You.

Trust in the LORD forever, for the LORD GOD is an everlasting rock."
(Isaiah 26:3-4, ESV)

In your world, who has an "anxious heart" and needs to hear kind words today? Will you be the one to speak them?

Asking for a Longer Bungee Cord

Proverbs 13:12. **"Hope deferred makes the heart sick, but a desire fulfilled is a tree of life.** (ESV)"

Bungee cords are designed to stretch easily and hold objects down safely in all sorts of applications. We've all seen them utilized to secure bikes, suitcases, ladders or even surf boards to car-tops.

We all encounter disappointments. In the "world you will have tribulation," Jesus explained. In the face of difficulty, disappointment or delay some people abandon hope. Or they grow weary of having anything resembling a good expectation. To them it becomes emotionally easier not to anticipate anything rather than to risk having their desires dashed again and again. Sometimes we can even find ourselves hoping for what we want to happen rather than for what God has actually promised.

Like a bungee cord, God-given hope will stretch to hold the true promises of God tightly to our heart. Remember what the Lord did for Abraham in giving him a son, Isaac, after twenty-five years of waiting. God gave Samuel to Hannah after years of "stretching." In the great parable the father looked long for the return of his prodigal son.

The truth is that Christ has made many promises to us, including: He is always with us. He will never leave us. He will cause us to triumph ultimately. He will work all things together for good finally. Above all our relationship with Christ is held secure by God continually. "For I am sure," Paul wrote, "that neither death, nor life, nor angels, nor rulers, nor things present, nor things to come, nor powers, nor height, nor depth, nor anything else in all creation, will be able to separate us from the love of God, in Christ Jesus our Lord." (Matthew 28:20; Hebrews 13:5; 2 Corinthians 2:14; Romans 8:28; 8:38-39, ESV)

Our greatest hope ever remains the Lord's return! "For the grace of God has appeared, bringing salvation for all people, training us to renounce ungodliness and worldly passions, and to live self-controlled, upright, and godly lives in the present age, waiting for our blessed hope, the appearing of the glory of our great God and Savior Jesus Christ. . . . . Let us hold fast the confession of our hope without wavering, for he who promised is faithful." (Titus 2:11-13; Hebrews 10:23, ESV)

Yes, "deferred" hope affects us but only temporarily. When our load is too large and we run out of godly expectation we can ask Jesus Christ for a longer bungee. The more centered we become upon Christ and His desires for us, the more our hopes will be fulfilled as a tree of life.

Wise Contentment v. Envy

Proverbs 14:30. "A tranquil heart gives life to the flesh, but envy makes the bones rot. (ESV)"

I struggle with wire-grass in my lawn. It's prolific. It grows into borders in no time. It re-roots everywhere it goes. You have to keep pulling and keep pulling it up as you go along. It's invasive.

Envy is a species of "wire-grass" in the soul. It has the tendency to intertwine with practically everything. More specifically it chokes out the best of Christ-focused contentment.

Satan appealed to envy when speaking to Eve. He convinced her that God had denied her something essential -- something she should desire and possess. You know the result.

King Ahab envied Naboth's vineyard. Jezebel, the king's notoriously wicked wife, had Naboth killed so that her husband could possess what he desired. For God, that was the last straw! In that very vineyard, on the very land Naboth walked on in security and pleasure only days earlier, Elijah met Ahab and prophesied the king's death in judgment. (1 Kings 21)

Remember! Jesus Christ was crucified because of the envy of the Jewish leaders! Even the apostolic band broke into arguments over who should have the preeminent place. Corinth, the early church in southern Greece, did the same. And jealousy has re-rooted itself throughout church history.

The very thing we envy is death to us. Our decision is either to die to the object of our envy and live for Christ; or to live for the object and die somewhat to Christ.

Be ruthless with your own "wire-grass." For Christ's sake love those whom God has blessed with the very thing you envy. Show a new resolve and thank God, only wise, that He has granted this favor to them but <u>not</u> to you at this time. All this leads to a "sound heart" -- one that loves and trusts the Creator rather than the creation to meet every legitimate need.

Wisdom and Prayer:

Proverbs 15:8. "The sacrifice of the wicked is an abomination to the LORD, but the prayer of the upright is His delight. (NAU)"

Walking through the dense woods at Camp David, Ronald Reagan could often be seen bending over, picking up acorns and placing them in a sack for the return trip to Washington. The President enjoyed feeding the fortunate squirrels in the White House Rose Garden.

A. C. Lyles, a Hollywood producer and long-time Reagan friend, was present one afternoon in the Oval Office. In relaxed conversation with the President, Lyles heard an odd scratching sound emanating from a glass door facing the Rose Garden. Looking that way Lyles caught sight of a squirrel standing on its hind legs and peering in. Without a word Reagan rose and collected some acorns from a nearby pack. He opened the door and then tossed several handfuls into the garden.

Somehow those White House squirrels had learned to identify the availability of tasty acorns with "the big man in the building." When they experienced need they boldly came up and scratched on the door. Never mind that Ronald Regan was one of the most powerful authorities on earth!

Be assured that the Heavenly Father not only hears our prayers but also anticipates them. He has graciously provided for all our legitimate needs (as He defines them) with a meticulous care that should boggle the imagination. And without question God enjoys it when we come boldly and "scratch" at the door of His throne room, peering in and waiting in anticipation for Him. "Let us then with confidence draw near to the throne of grace, that we may receive mercy and find grace to help in time of need." (Hebrews 4:16, ESV)

Wisdom encourages us to take all of life to God in prayer and then take all that God offers back into life. Prayer is one sure indicator that godly wisdom is present and functioning properly in our lives.

What situation, what requests, would the Lord have you to bring before Him this day of His amazing grace? ". . . for your Father knows what you need before you ask him." (Matthew 6:8, ESV)

Overcoming Spiritual Vertigo

Proverbs 16:2. "All the ways of a man are clean in his own sight, but the LORD weighs the motives. (NAU)"

Sometimes in the early days of flight when thick weather enveloped a plane, a pilot would inextricably fly the machine straight into the ground. As it turned out the problem was not mechanical but a matter of human misperception. Flyers were developing vertigo.

Engineers tackled the difficulty and developed new means of measurement. Dials were fitted in the cockpit; one displayed the relationship of the plane to the horizon (i.e., the ground), another indicated altitude, etc. Through meticulous training, pilots stopped relying on their own perceptions and entrusted their wellbeing to mechanical instrumentation.

Jesus taught us: "without Me you can do nothing!" This means we can't properly assess our lives, neither our successes nor our failures, apart from the Lord! God alone is capable of weighing inward motives as well as outward actions. On occasion we assume we're "flying" fine when in fact we're headed straight for the ground. When we live by our own wits and wisdom we tend to be swift to judge others and quick to justify ourselves. This proverb gives us pause on both accounts.

In Psalm 139, David humbly asks: "Search me, O God, and know my heart! Try me and know my thoughts! And see if there be any grievous way in me, and lead me in the way everlasting!" (23-24, ESV) When our thoughts run to self-congratulations or when we undergo character assessment it's important to keep these verses front and center. Christ is not interested in how we "seem" to ourselves. Instead we're to glance often at our "instruments", at God's Word and the input of His Spirit, and then make needed adjustments in order to stay on course.

"For by the grace given to me I say to everyone among you not to think of himself more highly than he ought to think, but to think with sober judgment." (Romans 12:3, ESV)

"For the word of God is living and active, sharper than any two-edged sword, piercing to the division of soul and of spirit, of joints and of marrow, and discerning the thoughts and intentions of the heart. And no creature is hidden from His sight, but all are naked and exposed to the eyes of Him to whom we must give account." (Hebrews 4:12-13, ESV)

The One Godly "Cover-up"

Proverbs 17:9. "Whoever covers an offense seeks love, but he who repeats a matter separates close friends. (ESV)"

It's not always necessary to bring to light the story of someone's fall into darkness. So we should certainly question our own motivations any time we feel inclined to "repeat" the sins of others. It's one thing to confess our own faults but quite another to confess the faults of others. When we shame others we shame ourselves.

Here's the love of Christ displayed, to bring the struggling individual out of the problem rather than bringing the details of the struggle out to others. This Scripture doesn't encourage minimizing or ignoring the wrong either. The love of Jesus "covers" the one in transgression with any or all of the following: private counsel, personal correction, pertinent wisdom, pleas for repentance, and the renewing of faith, hope and love.

Recall how Jesus Christ, our Great High Priest, operates! "And before Him no creature is hidden, but all are naked and laid bare to the eyes of the One to whom we must render an account . . . . For we do not have a high priest who is unable to sympathize with our weaknesses, but we have One who in every respect has been tested as we are, yet without sin. Let us therefore approach the throne of grace with boldness, so that we may receive mercy and find grace to help in time of need . . . . He is able to deal gently with the ignorant and wayward, since He himself is subject to weakness." (Hebrews 4:13, 15-5:2, NRS)

Jesus "ever lives to make intercession for us"; shouldn't we follow His lead and intercede always – exposing rarely?

Humility before Honor

Proverbs 18:12. "Before destruction the heart of man is haughty, but humility goes before honor. (NAU)"

On the many occasions when we struggle with thinking too highly of ourselves there is an easy remedy available. We simply behold Christ. "A sight of God's glory humbles," Thomas Watson wrote, just as the "stars vanish when the sun appears." Now that's the vanishing act that God desires to see!

It's unlikely you'll ever see this series of books:

Humility, Vol. 1 (650 pages)
Humility, Vol. 2 (543 pages)
Humility, Vol. 3 (508 pages)

Because if you've got that much to say about humility you probably don't have it in sufficient supply! Only Jesus can 'write the book' on meekness; and He's decided to write it in you and me:

"Do nothing from selfishness or empty conceit, but with humility of mind regard one another as more important than yourselves; do not merely look out for your own personal interests, but also for the interests of others."

"Have this attitude in yourselves which was also in Christ Jesus, who, although He existed in the form of God, did not regard equality with God a thing to be grasped, but emptied Himself, taking the form of a bond-servant, and being made in the likeness of men."

"Being found in appearance as a man, He humbled Himself by becoming obedient to the point of death, even death on a cross. For this reason also, God highly exalted Him, and bestowed on Him the name which is above every name, so that at the name of Jesus every knee will bow, of those who are in heaven and on earth and under the earth, and that every tongue will confess that Jesus Christ is Lord, to the glory of God the Father." (Philippians 2:3-11, NAU)

Christ calls us to humble ourselves but He also humbles us. Before Jesus honored His disciples, He made sure, `certified' if you will, an acceptable degree of humility. He did it with Joseph. He did with Moses. He did it with Elijah. He did it with Peter. He did it with John. He did it with Paul. He did it with Martha and He'll do it with us.

Actually, it does seem that Jesus Christ is turning out a multi-volume work on humility – a separate book on each of His disciples. And this question remains. How far along, how many pages has Jesus written on the subject of meekness in your life? One thing we know for sure, the honor for what is penned thus far belongs entirely to the Author and not to the book!

Enjoying the Supremacy of Jesus Christ

Proverbs 19:23. "The fear of the Lord leads to life and whoever has it rests satisfied; he will not be visited with harm. (ESV)"

Before my friends or I knew what was going on spiritually, we'd pretty much concluded that Jesus was unique and to be respected. In our perception, Christianity expounded many great moral principles but we spoke pejoratively about religion in general.

To us those odd religious folks added too many man-made rules that infringed upon any good time activity. In agreement with the skeptic, H. L. Mencken, we thought that one of the chief delights of these Christian-types was finding something new to add to an already long list of "don'ts."*

One of my close friends summarized things in this bit of "helpful" insight: "You know what? Church is made up of a bunch of little `bitty' grandmotherly-types with their small black pocket-books getting together once a week and sitting in a circle for some mind-numbing, boring prayer meeting." We all laughed and agreed.

And here things turn odd. For within a year of these strong assertions, there we sat in a circle and praying! It wasn't long before we found ourselves gladly praying with a number of those "grandmotherly"-types – and learning from them as well!

What happened? Jesus happened. The real fear of the Lord happened. Salvation happened. Perceptions changed, attitudes altered and it all made perfect sense. Wrong stuff starting falling away from our lifestyle or we gladly threw it away. These formerly cherished habits no longer brought "life" but undermined it!

I had more joy on many, many days not doing anything but just being associated with Christ than I had on my "best days" before! Talk about being "satisfied"!

What happened? I'm still not sure I understand. But I do know it's all centered in the person of the Lord Jesus Christ and in respecting His Word and receiving His exceeding love. There's nothing else in this world or the world to come like the Supremacy of Jesus.

* Actually, Mencken is reported to have defined a Puritan as someone who lay awake at night, fretting that somebody, somewhere, was having a good time.

The Unexpected "Path" to Honor

Proverbs 20:3. "It is an honor for a man to keep aloof from strife, but every fool will be quarreling. (ESV)"

The camera had captured two mountains goats for a nature documentary on an infinitesimally narrow path near the edge of sheer cliffs. The goats rounded a bend and came upon each other hundreds of feet above anything approaching level ground. There was no room to pass. The situation defined the word, dilemma.

The two continued to close the distance with no apparent concern. The narrator described the danger and built real suspense. Suddenly one goat dropped to his knees and then scrunched down as low as possible. Goat Number Two simply walked right over him and onto the path on the other side. In a moment all was normal and they both went right on their way.

When we're too sensitive about our own "honor" we generally bring dishonor to Jesus Christ. Strife is often fed by an inflated view of self-importance. Hence, "only by pride comes contention." When our imagined "honor" is at stake our fighting is always with "flesh and blood."

The New Testament issues this warning: "but if you bite and devour one another, watch out that you are not consumed by one another." (Galatians 5:15, ESV) The positive injunction goes like this: "Let all bitterness and wrath and anger and clamor, and slander be put away from you, along with all malice: be kind one to another, tenderhearted, forgiving one another, as God in Christ forgave you." (Ephesians 4:31-32, ESV)

It is the grace of God that enables us to cut down on relational friction by taking the more humble posture. With your spouse, with your family members, with your co-workers, with your friends, with the store clerk, with the less than competent driver and with all others, will you honor the Lord by identifying and terminating your argumentative ways? May

109

Jesus bring increasing honor on your life as you defer to His all-surpassing honor in all things both small and great .

The Triumphant Christ

Proverbs 21:30-31. **"There is no wisdom and no understanding and no counsel against the LORD. The horse is prepared for the day of battle, but victory belongs to the LORD.** (NAU)"

Anything multiplied by 0 = 0. The combined intelligence and resources of the world aligned against God = nothing.

From the first moment Jesus opened His infant eyes on this dark world to the last second when He closed His dying eyes on the cross, the devil and those aligned with him schemed and struck against The Messiah.

Hearing that Christ was born in Bethlehem, Herod attempted to kill Jesus. Satan, in the wilderness of temptation, purposed to overthrow the faith of the Son of God. Even the hometown people of Nazareth tried to stone Jesus at the commencement of his ministry.

The Pharisees, the Doctors of the Law, and the Sadducees did all to trap Him in His words, to dissuade people from following Him, to contradict His teaching and awesome works, to disbelieve His miracles, to overthrow His popularity, to arrange to have Him killed and finally to witness the crucifixion. The Romans acquiesced in the trial, scourging and crucifying Jesus. By 3 p.m. that afternoon at the cross it appeared that their combined "wisdom, insight and plan" against the Lord had succeeded. Not so . . . Sunday was yet to come!

Jesus triumphed over them in every respect: He was raised from the dead. In fact God used their very scheming and striking against The Messiah as the means to bring about their own defeat and the redemption for many more.

This triumph of Jesus was predicted a 1,000 years before He came. "Why are the nations in an uproar and the peoples devising a vain thing? The kings of the earth take their stand and the rulers gather together against the Lord and against His Anointed One . . . . He who sits in the heavens laughs, The Lord scoffs at them. Then He will speak to them in His anger and terrify them in His fury: 'But as for Me, I have installed My King upon Zion, My holy mountain.'" (Psalm 2:1-2, 4-6, NAU)

What was true for Jesus, He has made true for His followers. Multiply anything by 0 and you get 0. No "wisdom, insight or effort" against us from any source will succeed. "Greater is He who is in you than he who is in the world." (1 John 4:4, NAU) Now we have become "more than conquerors through Him who loved us . . . [and] neither death nor life, neither angels nor principalities, nor present things, nor things to come, nor powers, neither height, nor depth, nor any other created thing, will be able to separate us from the love of God which is in Christ Jesus our Lord." (Romans 8:37ff, ESV and NAU).

Hallelujah . . . Maranantha. Does your outlook and demeanor reflect the reality of a triumphant Messiah today?

Wisdom's Riveting Focus on Eternity

Proverbs 22:2. "The rich and poor meet together: the LORD is the Maker of them all. (NAU)"

In light of this verse take a look at the poem "Southern Pacific" (1918) by Carl Sandburg. While reading the following stanzas remember that Collis Huntington (1821-1900) was one of the wealthiest men of the time and owning both the Southern Pacific and Central Pacific railroads. Note the "leveling" effect of death.

Huntington sleeps in a house six feet long.
Huntington dreams of railroads he built and owned.
Huntington dreams of 10,000 men saying: Yes, sir.

Blithery sleeps in a house six feet long.
Blithery dreams of rails and ties he laid.
Blithery dreams of saying to Huntington: Yes, sir.

Huntington.
Blithery, sleep in houses six feet long.

We live with frequent reminders of the mortality reality. Perhaps that's why Richard Baxter* advised: "Preach as a dying man to dying men." The wisdom of God affirms to young and old alike, male and female, rich and poor and educated and under-educated: Use this life to prepare for the next.

"We are of good courage, I say, and prefer rather to be absent from the body and to be at home with the Lord. Therefore we also have as our ambition, whether at home or absent, to be pleasing to Him. For we must all appear before the judgment seat of Christ, so that each one may be recompensed for his deeds in the body, according to what he has done, whether good or bad." (2 Corinthians 5:8-10, NAU)

Will you establish a means through which you can be reminded of eternal priorities -- perhaps by memorizing select verses that address our life here and all it entails as brief while also stressing the far surpassing value of things eternal?

* The Puritan pastor of Kiddeminster, England.

The Motivation to Please

Proverbs 23:24-25. "The father of the righteous will greatly rejoice; he who fathers a wise son will be glad in him. Let your father and mother be glad; let her who bore you rejoice. (ESV)"

To inspire gladness in those who love us most, that's the heart of a wise son or daughter developing as it should.

In teenage years that perspective will certainly see an adjustment. The divine design for that critical season of life is . . . that we grow in the desire to inspire gladness in the heavenly Father by our choices and character. This greater God-ward focus doesn't erase a secondary desire to be a blessing to earthly parents either.

Jesus knows that time of transition only too well. At age twelve the Son of God made this statement to his parents, Mary and Joseph: "Did you not know that I must be in my Father's house?" (Luke 2:49, ESV) Later Jesus explained His greatest ruling principle and passion in life, the core of His spotless heart: "I do always those things that please" the Father. (John 8:29, ESV)

Perhaps you're saying, "Yea, but that's typically <u>not</u> what happens. In my life, and in the lives of others, the transition is not from pleasing parents to pleasing the Lord, but rather to pleasing ourselves in most everything. The `self-root' immerges during this stage and seeks domination."

This world may consider that development as entirely "normal" but not God. The Lord sees the shift for what it is; the likeness of Satan growing in us and whose ultimate principle is pleasing Numero Uno. When we habitually aim to prefer SELF, "it profits us nothing."

This nature is in need of redemption. In saving us through Jesus Christ, God takes us down to the grave. And then He raises us up with the Son that we may act like His children. The great principle and passion now becomes to "to walk in a manner worthy of the Lord fully pleasing to Him, bearing fruit in every good work." And to remember this old exhortation as well: "Children, obey your parents in everything, for this pleases the Lord." (Colossians 1:10; 3:20, ESV)

Consider who it is that you are most seeking to please today? "Finally, then, brothers, we ask and urge you in the Lord Jesus, that as you received from us how you ought to live and to please God, just as you are doing, that you do so more and more." (1 Thessalonians 4:1, ESV)

Knocked Down but Not Out

Proverbs 24:16. "For a righteous man may fall seven times and rise again, but the wicked shall fall by calamity. (NKJ)"

Jesus renamed Simon calling him Peter – meaning a stone. Yet at times Peter appeared to be a rolling stone and rolling downhill at that. But that's not the end of the story.

Before it was over, when others were falling down, Peter was standing tall for the Lord. He was holding others up as well and offering encouragement for those who were stumbling. Eventually, the man became a solid rock – in fact a martyr for Jesus Christ.

How many times was this apostle "flattened" in developing a truly triumphant faith? Peter made a career out of getting back up: after flailing in the Sea of Galilee, after failing to understand the necessity of the cross ("Get you behind Me, Satan!"), after attempting to detain the Lord Jesus on the Mount of Transfiguration, and after denying the Lord three times the night before the crucifixion. Simon was not among those present with Jesus at the cross (Matthew 14; 16; 17; 26)

How the resurrection of Jesus resuscitated the leading apostle! It became the difference between being "knocked down" and being "knocked out"! This proverb signifies that Peter's experience with sinking faults was in some ways typical. A just person may be flattened repeatedly. Yet Christ enables us to get back up and out of habitual sins, out of relational rejection, or arise from the dire affects of circumstantial difficulties and even full-scale demonic attacks.

Christians, while standing for the Lord Jesus, are no mere passive spectators but determined participators in the grand spiritual battle of the ages: "Wherefore take unto you the whole armor of God, that you

may be able to withstand in the evil day, and having done all, to stand."
(Ephesians 6:13, KJV)

Through the Holy Spirit, God will empower us to stand up for Him. "Be strong and courageous. Do not be frightened, and do not be dismayed, for the LORD your God is with you wherever you go." (Joshua 1:9, ESV) The next time you are knocked over, remember these words of Jesus: "Lazarus! Come forth!" If we are to learn to stand for Him we must learn to stand through Him.

Plain Faith and a Great Mystery

Proverbs 25:2. "It is the glory of God to conceal things, but the glory of kings is to search things out. (ESV)"

I don't think I've adequately appreciated the great mysteries involving faith. I'm probably not alone.

Whereas the Word presents a complicated reality, the contemporary church seems more concerned with simplifying reality – shaping it for our purposes. What is deemed spiritually pragmatic, plain and practical is judged to be of the highest value.

If certain contemporaries had written the Bible, things might have been arranged far differently. No longer Genesis, Exodus, Leviticus . . . Matthew, Mark, Luke and John. No longer truth scattered here and there and much in narrative, story-telling form. But a convenient topical arrangement – resembling more of a "seminar" approach.

We'd have concise books entitled: How to Believe in Jesus, How to Discover Purpose, How to Be Fulfilled in Marriage, How to Raise Godly Children, Basic Beliefs, How to Grow a Church, Overcoming Childhood Hurts, Managing Conflict Rather than Letting Conflict Manage You, Developing an Effective Prayer Life, How to Encounter, Endure and Benefit from Trials, Using Money Wisely, Debating the Second Coming, etc.

It would, no doubt, all be quite catchy and thoroughly organized. We wouldn't have Leviticus either – it would be part of the appendix under, "Ancient Rituals of the Old Testament."

Of one thing I'm certain . . . our New Revised Seminar Study Bible would be devoid of all mystery. We would consciously avoid topics that confuse or puzzle us – or that require more than a nanosecond of searching and thinking.

Yet this remains! "It is the glory of God to conceal a thing." Those elements of mystery show us His surpassing greatness. They emphasize His transcendence and make us grateful for what is made plain. What takes longer for us to grasp typically has a good affect. We're called to a heart pursuit, not just a head pursuit of Jesus Christ. The remaining mysteries of faith challenge us to search more fully. In actuality, without an awareness of mystery we cannot properly define or adequately live in God's reality.

The seminar is a practical place for explaining certain elements of life and faith. But we aren't called to worship as a seminar! We're called to worship as the church for what we already know AND with awe for what is beyond. "Because we are members of His body. This mystery is profound, and I am saying that it refers to Christ and the church." (Ephesians 5:30, 32, ESV)

A Graphic Analogy
Depicting Foolishness

Proverbs 26:11. "Like a dog that returns to his vomit is a fool who repeats his folly. (ESV)"

The devil promised high: "You will be as gods." But the result was to bring us low -- leaving the entire race "like a dog that returns to his vomit."

The fall resulted in the corruption of our nature. It was vile in that first offense and vile in the constant repetition of offenses since then. Not only have "all sinned" and come short of God's glory, but all have sinned in the same way numerous times . . . "like a dog that returns to his vomit."

This disgusting image and analogy (but given by God Himself!) leaves us groping for His help. How could we be attracted back to the very thing that one hour ago, or one day ago, or one week ago, or one month ago, made us quite "ill."

Realizing the appetites of the flesh we stop and pray with Paul: "O wretched man that I am! who shall deliver me from the body of this death?" (Romans 7:24, KJV) In answer, the Letter to the Romans brings the best of news. For God will not only justify us through the blood and righteousness of Jesus Christ but also free us from sin-tyranny. And He will not leave His work until it's finished; and He will not finish His work until we are as "sheep returning to the pasture."

There's hope in Jesus for dealing with every disgusting and addictive way we think, feel, speak and act. "Gad, a troop shall tramp upon him, but he shall triumph at last." (Genesis 49:19, NKJ) It is the power of the Holy Spirit that reforms our desires and transforms our "tastes" for new and better things.

Regarding your life, identify some repeated ungodly motive, thought, word or behavior. Bring it afresh to Christ today. Pray not only for forgiveness but also for solid triumph! "If we confess our sins, He is faithful and just to forgive us our sins AND to cleanse us from all unrighteousness." (1 John 1:9, ESV)

We can sing, "be of sin the double cure, save from wrath and make me pure."

Self-Flattery is Repugnant

Proverbs 27:2. "Let another praise you and not your own mouth; a stranger and not your own lips. (ESV)"

In the 1950's my favorite uncle, Laird Loftis, was the American marketing officer for British Airways Corporation. From a kid's perspective that was pretty cool because he lived in New York City, traveled overseas and brought us back great gifts.

One winter evening Laird attended a fancy dinner party in New York. Someone present had the reputation of always talking about the "important" people he'd met and conversed with including the governor, the CEO, the great athlete, and so on. There was also a dentist, another of my uncle's friends, present that night.

Near the end of the meal the guest with the somewhat inflated ego was in fine form, dominating conversation. As the monologue continued Laird noticed the dentist across the table bend over as if to pick up a napkin or fork. Then a few moments later he did the same thing again. He repeated the motion so often you'd have thought he was trying to eat peas with a knife or that it was time for after-dinner calisthenics.

Finally the distracted conversationalist asked, "Doc, what on earth are you doing over there bending down under the table?"

"Well," the dentist quipped, "I'm just picking up all of those names you've been dropping the last few minutes!" [Spontaneous group laughter.]

Self-flattery can assume many forms and disguises. Sometimes it is manifested in overt verbal self-praise. At other times it sneaks into our unexpressed thoughts. What's up when we align ourselves closely with those we consider especially "important" people and remind others of the fact? Inappropriate self-flattery might even appear when we engage in hyper-criticism of others. There's no virtue in attempting to build ourselves up by bringing other people down.

It's good to remember that the Lord did not seek "His own glory" but the honor of His Father (John 8:50). Jesus spent much time and energy with those considered "nobodies" by a majority. He spent less time with the spiritual snobs. His interaction with religious self-flatterers always resulted in friction. Our pride rubs Christ the wrong way.

The New Testament offers us this pointed exhortation: "Do not be haughty, but associate with the lowly. Never be conceited." (Romans 12:16, ESV) Ask Jesus Christ to enable you to detect and then guard your heart against all the various forms of unwise self-praise.

Happiness vs. Hardness

Proverbs 28:14. "Blessed is the one who fears the LORD always, but whoever hardens his heart will fall into calamity. (ESV)"

Satan hopes for hardness of heart. It makes his job a whole lot easier.

The archenemy of Jesus started with Adam and Eve in the Garden. He boldly questioned the need for continued expressions of reverent love for the Heavenly Father. It worked! For our first parents hardened their hearts and "fell" into calamity.

The Devil will use any opportunity to mix his demonic brand of "concrete" into our soul. It's time to watch carefully when we experience:

- hard circumstances
- or disappointments that are hard to swallow
- or when we encounter hardened religious people
- or Christians that will hardly give us the time of day.

Satan is an expert at distorting our image of God – so that the Lord comes off as untrustworthy and the One against whom we should perhaps harden our heart. Short of that, the devil will encourage that same hardened response against fellow Christians.

Sooner or later (and sometimes sooner and later) life gets difficult. That's beyond question. The real query is, "Will we harden our heart in the process?" Some are in that season of testing right now.

Remember the promise, "Blessed is the one who fears the LORD always"; and the exhortation of Paul to Timothy: "You therefore, my son, be strong in the grace that is in Christ Jesus. Suffer hardship with me as a good soldier of Jesus Christ." (2 Timothy 2:1, 3, NAU)

Definitely remember Job, who experienced enough hardships for all of us combined: "As an example of suffering and patience, beloved, take the prophets who spoke in the name of the Lord. Indeed we call blessed those who showed endurance. You have heard of the endurance of Job and you have seen the purpose of the Lord, how the Lord is compassionate and merciful." (James 5:10-11, NRS)

Our happiness in Christ is protected by a constant experience of reverent gratefulness for and respectful trust in Jesus. He will not abandon or forsake us! There is a deep-seated experience of happiness in God that is neither derived from nor dependent upon favorable circumstances but directed by Christ Himself who is above all and with us in all.

Drawing Circles and Lines

Proverbs 29:27. "An unjust man is an abomination to the righteous, but one whose way is straight is an abomination to the wicked. (ESV)"

It's assumed and rightly so, that God's love teaches us how to draw larger and more inclusive circles that embrace many people. Yet Christ also instructs us by drawing very precise lines defining His standards and that separate people. Wisdom rebuffs every false form of tolerance that disallows any moral criterion. The Holy Spirit guides us as to when we should be drawing a circle and when we should be drawing a line.

The church intercedes that God would save all sorts of people and include them in a circle of prayer. But regarding righteousness, we are not to give an inch. We are to make no compromises. Those who disregard His teachings are on one side of that holy line and those who follow Jesus are called to be on the other. For us to exercise discernment and make a decision as to which side of the line we should be on does not violate the "judge-not" principle.

On occasion it's even necessary to draw lines among professing Christians: "I wrote to you in my letter not to associate with sexually immoral people," the apostle Paul wrote, "not at all meaning the sexually immoral of this world, or the greedy and swindlers, or idolaters, since then you would need to go out of the world.

"But now I am writing to you not to associate with anyone who bears the name of brother if he is guilty of sexual immorality or greed, or is an idolater, reviler, drunkard, or swindler -- not even to eat with such a one. For what have I to do with judging outsiders? Is it not those inside the church whom you are to judge? God judges those outside. `Purge the evil person from among you.'" (1 Corinthians 5:9-13, ESV)

New Testament church discipline (not an oxymoron) is not done for punitive purposes but in hopes of amendment and re-inclusion. Notice that the immediate means for restoration is not the drawing of a circle but the redrawing of a line of demarcation. The message to the offender is that safety can only be found on the Lord's side of the boundary.

We are quite dependent on the Lord Jesus and His wisdom as to when to pen the circle and when to sketch out the line. One point of this proverb is that we should be disgusted over certain behaviors on the other side of the boundary and of the people who do them.

Putting the Fragile in the Unbreakable

Proverbs 30:24, 26. "**Four things on earth are small, but they are exceedingly wise: . . . . the rock badgers are a people not mighty, yet they make their homes in the cliffs.** (ESV)"

Rock Badgers operate with God-designed instinctive awareness. Their protection and preservation come not from within but from without. They've become experts in hiding the fragile in the unbreakable -- their bodies and families among the strong rocks. When danger threatens they hightail it back to the boulders.

Theologians divide the church into the "church-triumphant" consisting of those who have died in Christ and already entered heaven, and the "church-militant" consisting of those who remain in the heat of the battle still warring for Christ.

Thus our pressing need in this present world is for divine protection. At times, attacks will become acute. King David knew how to bring his own "fragile" life to the Lord: "My soul, wait in silence for God only, for my hope is from Him. He only is my rock and my salvation, my stronghold; I shall not be shaken. On God my salvation and my glory rest; the Rock of my strength, and my refuge, is in God. Trust in him at all times, O people; pour out your heart before him; God is a refuge for us." (Psalm 62:5-8, NAU)

We're also assured that Jesus is using circumstances, and especially difficulties, to expose our weaknesses and provide His strength. Will we trust in ourselves? That path leads us into deception? Will we trust in the power of external entities? That leads us into the path of fear? Or will we trust implicitly in the Jesus? That leads us forward into greater faith and security?

In learning to place the "fragile in the unbreakable," Martin Luther, whose life was put in real jeopardy for the Word of Christ, found the protection we must also seek:

A mighty fortress is our God
A bulwark never failing
Our helper He amid the flood
Of mortal ills prevailing
For still our ancient foe
Doth seek to work us woe
His craft and power are great
And armed with cruel hate
On earth is not His equal

Did we in our own strength confide
Our striving would be losing
Were not the right Man on our side
The Man of God's own choosing
Dost ask who that may be?
Christ Jesus, it is He
Lord Sabaoth, His Name
From age to age the same
And He must win the battle

The Timeless Pattern for Godly Women

Proverbs 31, The Virtuous Woman (Please read vss. 10-31)

The Virtuous Woman is described as "the wife of noble character." The passage remains wisdom's timeless "pattern" for developing a godly lady in every culture and in every generation. The attitudes and wisdom described can be extrapolated for all women (and for that matter all men).

This godly lady is living a joyful and productive life of character and faith. She's extraordinarily busy in a great variety of earthly projects and for divine reasons. In every role The Virtuous Woman is succeeding -- in every task she's progressing -- in every endeavor she's resourceful.

Where appropriate, she follows appropriately; and when appropriate, she leads appropriately. "Many women do noble things," the Bible states, "but you surpass them all."

What's her secret? Her agenda has little to do with personal "charm" and nothing to do with dependence on natural physical "beauty." Her life has everything to do with God and the relationships He has given to her: "but a woman who reverently and worshipfully fears the Lord, she shall be praised" (v. 30, Amplified Bible).

In our day, all sorts of feminine "patterns" contend for the soul. Strong and aggressive cultural forces are constantly touted and involve self-empowerment, self-realization, personal assertiveness, personal charm, and physical beauty. These core values place unreal pressures on women to set their own agenda and live out their personal dreams.

The overarching test for both women and men is whether we will be self-defined or defined by God Himself – molded by the world or molded by Christ. Proverbs 31 and indeed the entirety of Scripture provide us with THE "pattern" for followers of Christ. In stark contrast, it is always foolish to take our cue from the world. We are surrounded by constant pressures to conform to the dictates and values of this present generation. That is precisely the reason God gives us His own timeless Word and wisdom.

The Virtuous Woman, defined by God, stands graciously for Him and His truth. In following the pattern she has become the example. "Give her the reward she has earned, and let her works bring her praise at the city gate!" -- of the New Jerusalem that is!

Learning through Repetition

Proverbs 1:5-6. *"Let the wise listen to these proverbs and become even wiser. Let those with understanding receive guidance by exploring the meaning in these proverbs and parables, the words of the wise and their riddles. (NLT)"*

The world constantly moves on to new and different messages but remains inwardly the same. Disciples consistently reread the same words of Christ and are yet made different.

What we hear once we need to hear more than once. We should not expect to get every lesson on the first go-around. The apostle Paul affirmed this approach: "To write the same things to you is no trouble to me and is safe for you." (Philippians 3:1, ESV)

Even the best of biblical teachers remained lifelong learners and continued to study every possible source. Moses was taught by Jethro, Solomon by David, Elisha by Elijah, the apostles by Peter, and Apollos by Priscilla and Aquila (Exodus 18:17ff; The Book of Proverbs; 1 Kings; Acts 11:2ff; Acts 18:24-26).

To remain teachable is to remain Wisdom's disciple. To learn at present what we might need in days ahead provides us with sufficient time to absorb the lesson well. In stark contrast, hard-heads won't learn at the moment what they don't need in the moment. And when the time comes for that neglected lesson it won't be there. They'll fail and be left wondering why?

"Beloved," the apostle explained, "I am writing you no new commandment, but an old commandment that you had from the beginning. The old commandment is the word that you have heard. (1 John 2:7, ESV)"

And so we're starting another month in Proverbs and reading the same words through again. In a very real sense, it's the Bible that's reading us and preparing us for new challenges and fresh circumstances. "Let the wise listen to these proverbs and become even wiser."

The Ruling Voice of Christ

Proverbs 2:1, 5. "My son, if you accept my words and you store up with you my commands . . . then you will understand the fear of the LORD and the knowledge of God you will find. (Bruce Waltke, *The Book of Proverbs*)"

The old King James translators rendered the word, "store," in this verse as "hide" – "hide my commandments with you." With that in mind I considered the difference between "hide" and "store."

Do you use a flashlight very often? I don't. Last time I looked I had one on the shelf over the washer and dryer. When I need it, the batteries are invariably low. And more than once I've had to use the remaining light trying to locate spares!

In a sense the flashlight is "hidden" in that laundry room for occasional use. Maybe the power will go off, or maybe I'll need to find something outside at night. I've got a flashlight hidden away in the car too.

But that's not what it means to "hide" God's Word – to put it aside only for emergencies or other crisis occasions.

The meaning here is more along the lines of resupplying the local grocery store. Consider the amazing variety of items that occupy those shelves the next time you walk down the grocery aisles. The major stocking typically happens in off-hours, at night or in the very early morning when customers are few. That effort is part of a very deliberate and regular routine.

"My commands store up with <u>you</u>." How is your own daily "stocking" of your mind and heart going with reference to God's Word and the Ruling Voice of Jesus Christ? Are you finding what you need through the week when you are weak and need it? Are you regularly reading and even memorizing Scripture?

The First Psalm affirms this essential lesson: "his delight is in the law of the LORD, and on his law he meditates day and night." Psalm 119 states: "I have stored up your word in my heart, that I might not sin against you." (v. 11) Thomas Watson wrote: "Leave not off reading the Bible till you find your hearts warmed. Let it not only inform you but inflame you!"

Count on it! God's wisdom will always instruct us to return to God's Word and stock up.

Trust in God's very Good Hand

Proverbs 3:5-6. "Trust in the Lord with all your heart and do not lean on your own understanding. In all your ways acknowledge Him, and He will make straight your paths. (ESV)"

At age seventeen, Joseph came within an inch of being murdered by his own jealous brothers. Instead they sold him to passing slavers who in turn traded him to an Egyptian master. It wasn't long before Joseph became Potiphar's most trusted servant.

Yet, Joseph's trying season was not at an end. Potiphar's wife seduced the young man albeit unsuccessfully! Denied repeatedly, she then turned against Joseph and accused him of rape. As a result, he was unjustly jailed and yet soon became the warden's most trusted worker. Yes, the prisoner was running the prison.

Consider Joseph's early adulthood. He experienced family rejection on a grand scale followed by imprisonment on a trumped up charge. His trials came in successive battering waves. I'm not sure I'd have done anywhere near as well, but Joseph remembered God.

Then the great Pharaoh had two vivid dreams that seemingly forecast imminent events. His "spiritual" advisors could not decipher the night visions. Pharaoh became antsy. The king's butler stepped forward and suggested that ruler call for that remarkable Hebrew prisoner who had demonstrated a real knack for interpretation.

Quickly shuffled from the prison to the throne room, Joseph stood before the king and accurately predicted Egypt's immediate future. Pharaoh made the thirty year-old foreigner, Prime Minister. For seven years Joseph supervised the gathering and preserving of bountiful grain harvests. There followed the seven years of famine and Joseph oversaw the selling and distribution of the abundance.

One day Joseph looked up from his stat sheets and saw familiar faces. His brothers had traveled from Canaan to obtain grain. They did not recognize Joseph and he hid his identity as well. After a series of character tests the now exalted younger brother gave expression to the faith by which he persevered and prevailed during those dim and doleful years.

"I am Joseph," he exclaimed! His shocked brothers didn't answer him a word. He brought them near and reiterated, "I am Joseph your brother, whom you sold into Egypt. But now, do not therefore be grieved or angry with yourselves because you sold me here; for God sent me before you to preserve life . . . . and to save your lives by a great deliverance. So now it was not you who sent me here, but God." (Genesis 45:4-8, ESV)

I am not Joseph and neither are you. But we have the same God who is worthy of our deepest trust in all our circumstances. We're called then, especially in our most trying situations, to "acknowledge Him in all our ways" for He will surely "make our paths straight." Jesus Christ is in charge more than we know!

Remaining Responsive Children

Proverbs 4:1, 3-4. "Listen, my children, to a father's instruction and be attentive that you may gain insight . . . . When I was a son with my father, tender, and my mother's favorite, He taught me and said to me, `Let your heart hold fast my words: keep my commandments and live.' (NRS)"

Daniel Defoe (ca. 1661-1731) penned, *The Life and Adventures of Robinson Crusoe* in 1719. If you remember, it's the story of a hard-headed son who rejects his parent's repeated advice and then goes to sea. Eventually, the rebellious Crusoe becomes the sole survivor of a shipwreck and lives for nearly 30 years on a deserted island.

What you may not remember is that on that island Crusoe comes to repentance and belief in Jesus. Eventually he leads "Friday" (a native from the nearby coastland) to Christ as well. Defoe wrote this adventure book as a sort of extended Christian tract and especially for youth! (It's ironic then that the abridged versions almost always edit out the rich Christian message.)

In relating the moment of breaking and awakening, Crusoe is made to say: "I took up the Bible and began to read. Only having opened the book casually, the first words that occurred to me were these, `Call on Me in the day of trouble and I will deliver, and you shall glorify Me.' It was not long after I set seriously to this work [of reading Scripture] but I found my heart more deeply and sincerely affected with the wickedness of my past life."

"I was earnestly begging of God to give me repentance when it happened providentially, the very day that reading the Scripture I came to these words, `He is exalted a Prince and a Savior to give repentance and to give remission.' I threw down the book and with my heart as well as my hands lifted up to heaven in a kind of ecstasy of joy, I cried out aloud,

`Jesus, You son of David! Jesus, You exalted Prince and Savior, give me repentance!'

This was the first time that I could say in the true sense of the words that I prayed in all my life; for now I prayed with a sense of my condition and with a true Scripture view of hope founded on the encouragement of the Word of God; and from this time, I may say, I began to have hope that God would hear me. Now I looked back upon my past life with such horror and my sins appeared so dreadful that my soul sought nothing of God but deliverance from the load of guilt that bore down all my comfort.

"As for my solitary life, it was nothing. And I add this part here to hint to whoever shall read it, that whenever they come to a true sense of things, they will find deliverance from sin a much greater blessing than deliverance from affliction."

Robinson Crusoe affirms at its core the instruction of wisdom in Proverbs, "Hear, children, the instruction of a father." And when that is ignored, the only remedy is reconciliation to the Heavenly Father through the death and resurrection of His obedient Son, Jesus.

"Lead us not into Temptation"

Proverbs 5:7-9. "Now, O sons, listen to me, and do not depart from the words of my mouth. Keep your way far from her [the temptress], and do not go near the door of her house, lest you give your honor to others and your years to the merciless, do not go near the door of her house. (ESV)"

This proverb helps to differentiate between those temptations that come seeking us and those that we go seeking. Jesus Christ was tempted yet without sin. The devil initiated and came to tempt Him. He never sought out temptation. He never succumbed either.

To Generalize: the Bible affirms that all will be tempted. It'll come looking for us. Temptation in and of itself is not transgression. But we're reminded to avoid what puts us in the path of temptation - to ask God to "lead us not into temptation" - to make no "provision for the flesh to fulfill the lusts thereof." When it happens God will make a way of "escape." (Matthew 6; Romans 13; 1 Corinthians 10:13)

Martin Luther explained the difference between temptation and actual sin: "It's the difference between having a bird fly over your head and having a bird build a nest on your head."

To Individualize: we've all got our own "flock of birds" that flies overhead seeking nesting privileges. Like Abraham we're learning to drive away those ravenous birds of prey from all that which we've dedicated to God (Genesis 15).

Do nothing to increase the power of any temptation. For once you've taken a step onto the "path to her door" that pathway has already taken hold of you. The downward pull will increase exponentially as you approach ungodly attractions. Then if unhindered, sin can progress from a toe-hold to a foot-hold to a strong-hold.

So Wisdom advises us emphatically: "avoid it, pass not by it, turn from it and pass away." (Proverbs 4:15) To exercise great care in matters of the soul demonstrates great respect and reverence for God. We are to avoid even the "appearance of evil" (1 Thessalonians 5:22).

Identify today any place where you've essentially put out a "welcome mat" for temptation. Draw near to God and as you do, determine to reverse course regarding wrong enticements. Confess the temptation and new resolve to stand against it to a trusted confidant and pray together for divine results.

The Biblical "Ant-Farm"

Proverbs 6:6-8. "Go to the ant, O sluggard, observe her ways and be wise, which having no chief, officer or ruler, prepares her food in the summer and gathers her provision in the harvest. (NAU)"

While we have nothing to teach ants and no means to teach them, these creatures have much to teach us. Ants don't possess a "size" advantage but a "wise" advantage. They operate with instinctive forethought. They diligently prepare for a time of scarcity in a time of plenty – and for the future in the present.

Joseph exhibited this same wisdom in Egypt: storing up the seven "good" years' harvest to take care of the seven "bad" years' famine. Noah before the flood was instructed by God and anticipated the coming judgment. He built a boat to survive the deluge while many people ridiculed the messenger and ignored the message. The five wise virgins rationed the use of their oil for the darkest watch at midnight to remain ready when the bridegroom appeared.

Many times Christ will instruct us: to delay present gratification, to persevere in working for Him now with hope for the future and to believe God's warnings of what's to come by preparing accordingly. On the flip side, it's amazing how some of the smartest and most successful individuals crawling around on the planet have made no preparation whatsoever for the life to come. Our connection with Jesus and His soon coming will result in present working:

"Therefore, my beloved brethren, be steadfast, immovable, always abounding in the work of the Lord, knowing that your toil is not in vain the Lord." (1 Corinthians 15:58, NAU)

"Therefore you also must be ready: for the Son of Man is coming at an hour you do not expect. Who then is a faithful and wise servant, whom his master has set over his household to give them their food at the proper time? Blessed is that servant, whom his master will find so doing when he comes." (Matthew 24:44-46, ESV)

Some of the most industrious workers, talented persons and diligent individuals are merely secularists. Spiritually, they're almost completely inactive. This proverb calls us out of this different sort of laziness as well.

Leaving the Saw in the Branch

Proverbs 7:1-2. "My son, keep my words and treasure up my commandments with you; keep my commandments and live. (ESV)"

It was the early afternoon of Sunday, December 7, 1941. Army Chief of Staff, General George C. Marshall, was at his Virginia home and climbed up on a ladder to prune a few limbs in his apple orchard.

The General had the saw blade roughly half-way through a larger branch when someone cried out from the house: "General! You have an urgent call from Washington!"

The Japanese had attacked Pearl Harbor. In the next weeks Marshall became instrumental in transforming the military from a peace-time to a war-time footing. For the remainder of WWII the General was invaluable in leading a two-ocean effort and presided over the greatest and farthest-reaching military campaign in history.

Finally, peace came in August 1945. One evening as Marshall and his wife were walking in the orchard the General looked up and spotted a rusted pruning saw half-way through an apple tree limb. Then he remembered December 7th. Greater priorities had eclipsed the lesser ones during the intervening years.

In the face of a rapidly degenerating world, in battle with awful demonic powers, and in confronting our own inward struggles, I ask you for Christ's sake: where do your priorities lie today? What "pruning saw" is God calling you to leave in the "branch" for a time? as you respond to Christ's greater challenge to know and make known His Word?

Why so much Preaching?

Proverbs, the whole of Chapter Eight (please crack open the Scripture and read)

Wisdom here stands at the crossroads, ascends the heights and preaches - exhorting us to listen in the strongest possible terms!

Throughout the ages the progress of the gospel, the progress of righteousness, the progress of wisdom, the progress of Christ-honoring holiness, the progress of all godly endeavors depends heavily on the progress of preaching.

Do we have a high view of preaching as the great God-ordained instrument that it is? Or have we become jaded or lethargic? When a culture, when a nation, when a movement, when a congregation, or when an individual turns away from preaching, the result is universally dire: "For this people's heart has grown dull, and with their ears they can barely hear, and their eyes they have closed, lest they should see with their eyes and hear with their ears and understand with their heart and turn, and I would heal them.'" (Matthew 13:15, ESV)

Christ's seven-time repeated heavenly exhortation resonates across church history: "He who has an ear, let him hear what the Spirit says to the churches." (Revelation, Chapters Two and Three)

Preaching is essential as these scriptures enforce:

"In those days John the Baptist came <u>preaching</u> in the wilderness of Judea." (Matthew 3:1, ESV) "The men of Nineveh will rise up at the judgment with this generation and condemn it, for they repented at the <u>preaching</u> of Jonah, and behold, something greater than Jonah is here." (Matthew 12:41, ESV) "Every day, in the temple and from house to house, they did not cease teaching and <u>preaching</u> Jesus as the Christ." (Acts 5:42, ESV)

Now to him who is able to strengthen you according to my gospel and the preaching of Jesus Christ, according to the revelation of the mystery that was kept secret for long ages but has now been disclosed and through the prophetic writings has been made known to all nations, according to the command of the eternal God, to bring about the obedience of faith - to the only wise God be glory forevermore through Jesus Christ! Amen." (Romans 16:25-27, ESV)

We are to attend preaching as much as possible; and pray for those who preach as fervently as possible; and listen to messages as carefully as possible; and implement Christ's wise counsel as consistently as possible. And may God, who makes all things possible, thereby bring about a greater awakening on this apostate continent.

Responding to a Gracious Invitation

Proverbs 9:4-6. "Whoever is simple, let him turn in here!" To him who lacks sense she [Wisdom] says , "Come, eat my bread and drink of the wine I have mixed. Leave your simple ways and live, and walk in the way of insight. (ESV)"

Who wouldn't admit that God, the Sovereign Creator and Ruler of the universe, has the prerogative to command us? We ARE surprised then to discover that God also "invites" us to follow Him and learn from Him. This strikes us as strange in the same way that it would be odd to be "invited" by our boss to do our work.

Yet here Wisdom invites us to learn as a fitting close to the introductory session of Proverbs (chapters 1-9). In a sense it's the kick-off banquet the night before classes begin! Think of your response if Bill Gates asked you to spend a season in Redmond, Washington and committed himself on a personal mentoring basis to pass on his career lessons? What if you could take a course in public speaking from Winston Churchill?

How much greater then is this invitation regarding wisdom to be valued and heeded! "Come to me, all who labor and are heavy laden," Jesus proclaimed, "and I will give you rest. Take my yoke upon you, and learn from me, for I am gentle and lowly in heart, and you will find rest for your souls." (Matthew 11:28-30, ESV)

The All-Sufficient God solicits empty and unfulfilled people to receive from His abundance: "Come, everyone who thirsts, come to the waters; and he who has no money, come, buy and eat! Come, buy wine and milk without money and without price. Why do you spend your money for that which is not bread, and your labor for that which does not satisfy? Listen diligently to me, and eat what is good, and delight yourselves in rich food." (Isaiah 55:1-2, ESV)

Incredibly, the Most Holy also invites sinners to be forgiven and cleansed: "'Come now, let us reason together,' says the LORD: 'though your sins are like scarlet, they shall be as white as snow; though they are red like crimson, they shall become like wool.'" (Isaiah 1:18, ESV)

Christ calls us to acknowledge our obvious need, leave our ways and in exchange to learn His wisdom! What will your answer be? "If any of you lacks wisdom, let him ask God, who gives generously to all without reproach, and it will be given him. (James 1:5, ESV)

All Spiritual Blessings

Proverbs 10:6. "Blessings are on the head of the righteous but the mouth of the wicked conceals violence. (ESV)"

It's amazing how we can use a word over and over and think we're 100% sure we know exactly what it means. The term "blessing" seems to fall into that category. For in reality it conveys much more than we comprehend and that's good news.

What else would we expect from the expression that describes heaven's permanent reality brought down to this fallen earth? Blessing describes what God lives in all the time and is willing to make our experience in following and obeying the Lord Jesus Christ.

Blessings on our "head" make us look up in growing awareness and gratefulness to Him from whom they derive. Go out tonight. Look into the vast expanse of the universe. You won't hear a voice. You won't see God. But He's present everywhere always. The Lord is obviously eternal, powerful and wise beyond all measure. Right behind the veil of this creation is the heaven in which God dwells. From that very place the Lord sent Jesus to redeem us.

We should conclude then that this world is best compared to a "Rest Stop" along the interstate. Go back inside. Now do you see how someone enduring some of the most difficult moments of life and the darkest hours can still admit, "I'm richly blessed."

John Paton and his wife, Mary Ann Paton, were pioneer missionaries to the New Hebrides islands of the Pacific. Not long after they moved to these remote coral isles Mary Ann became sick. She succumbed to island fever soon after giving birth to a child (who also died). Shortly before expiring someone asked Mary Ann if she regretted leaving her home in Scotland and coming so far away. Her reply was a Christian classic: "If

I had to do it all over again, I would do the same, but with far more pleasure, yes, with all my heart."

What a wonderful mystery is the reality of God's redeeming love that saves us, keeps us and fulfills us in time and eternity. "Blessed be the God and Father of our Lord Jesus Christ, who has blessed us with all spiritual blessings in heavenly places in Christ: according as he has chosen us in Him before the foundation of the world, that we should be holy and without blame before Him in love: having predestinated us unto the adoption of children by Jesus Christ to Himself, according to the good pleasure of His will, to the praise of the glory of His grace, wherein He has made us accepted in the beloved." (Ephesians 1:3-6, KJV)

The Both-Win Strategy

Proverbs 11:30. "The fruit of the righteous is a tree of life and he that wins souls is wise. (ESV)"

The American idea of "winning" is usually dominated by the "One Wins, Another Loses"-value system. And that can certainly be a part of biblical winning as well. David won and Goliath lost. Moses and the children of Israel prevailed at the Red Sea; Pharaoh and the Egyptians were obliterated. Jesus always triumphs. Satan is no victor.

So there's definitely a time in Christian experience for "One Wins, Another Loses": "I have written unto you, young men, because you are strong, and the word of God abides in you, and you have overcome the wicked one." (1 John 2:14, NKJ)

Yet winning works in another way as well: the "One Wins by Helping-Another-Win" concept. This proverb, "he that wins souls is wise," falls into that category of wisdom. For example, the home is no place for "One Wins - One Loses" (except in board games). If there's frequent strife and family members constantly asserting their rights, or ready to "win" conversations, or striving to get their way, or quick to put others in their place then God's wisdom is truly lacking.

James describes this stark contrast: "If you have bitter jealousy and selfish ambition in your hearts, do not boast and be false to the truth. This is not the wisdom that comes down from above, but is earthly, unspiritual, demonic. For where jealousy and selfish ambition exist, there will be disorder and every vile practice. But the wisdom from above is first pure, then peaceable, gentle, open to reason, full of mercy and good fruits, impartial and sincere. And a harvest of righteousness is sown in peace by those who make peace." (James 3:14-18, ESV)

The home's a place for the "Both Win" approach. It's the true husband and father who sacrificially leads and furthers the development, the godliness and happiness, of wife and children. (Ephesians 5:21-6:4) It's the righteous wife and mother who wins her husband and her children to faith in Jesus through her own heart and example of serving (1 Peter 3:1-4).

Does God create neighborhoods as a field for carnal competition to decide who has the best stuff, the brightest kids and the biggest bank account? "Love your neighbor as yourself" indicates a "Both Win" approach. The same should be said of the church and of all our associations and friendships (Philippians 2:3-4; Matthew 20:25-28).

So this question remains: Who will you be helping to win today? "He that wins souls is wise." That's a good description of the Lord Jesus Christ. When we follow Him, we also become a "tree of life."

Moral Debates and the Objective Rule of Scripture

Proverbs 12:5. "The thoughts of the righteous are right: but the counsels of the wicked are deceit. (KJV)"

All the current "debates" concerning moral standards in America, no matter the specific topic, bring up afresh the necessity of an absolute standard. We start by admitting that we're not God.

Humans are definitely not the ones who should be determining the standard. Ethics should never be approached as a smorgasbord with each group or individual autonomously deciding what is right and what is wrong. Instead, we should have every expectation that His Word will more frequently confront us than confirm us in aspects of our thinking. But that's good news. And we know we're on track when we find ourselves being newly conformed to what is written.

We should not come to Scripture then merely seeking its endorsement of our beliefs, our lifestyle choices or our agenda. This would be quite presumptuous, tantamount to putting our own thoughts above God's thoughts, our own words above God's words.

Those who utilize "counsels" of deceit will come to the Word looking for any angle that will affirm them in the preferences they already hold and take to Scripture. In that case people are looking for support more than the truth. As someone has succinctly put it, "If you come to the gospel picking and choosing what to accept and what to reject, it's no longer the gospel that you believe, but yourself."

It's not what we take to Christ's Word that counts, but what is revised through our interaction with Scripture and then taken from Him that really matters. The idea is summed up in this phrase, norma normans sed non normata – the norm that judges every other norm but is itself not judged by any other.

"Therefore I esteem right all Your precepts concerning everything, I hate every false way." (Psalm 119:128, NAU)

We do come to Scripture with the expectation that we'll be confronted in many areas of opinion, belief and lifestyle. We come knowing that trust and obedience will be required of us -- that the goal is to be conformed to its truth and teachings.

"For with You is the fountain of life; In Your light we see light." (Psalm 36:9, NAU)

"Your word is a lamp to my feet and a light to my path." (Psalm 119:105, NAU)

Words Reveal the Underlying Character

Proverbs 13:3. "Whoever guards his mouth preserves his life; he who opens wide his lips comes to ruin. (ESV)"

Many years ago while I was living in Richmond, Virginia, the James River spawned a strange algae. The H2O at home and everywhere else tasted like it had been soaking in a teenage boy's dirty socks. You quickly learned NOT to cut on the water.

It's the only time I've seen people standing in line to buy -- Bottled Water! A local park had a spigot tapped into an unaffected underground stream. Every day you had a "depression era" line of people waiting to fill up cans and containers.

The compassionate local merchants, hoping to lend a helping hand to the fine citizenry in their acute moment of crisis, jacked the price for water up to more than double. After two weeks or so it all cleared up and we avoided another French Revolution.

Everyone has said things they wish they hadn't. We've opened "wide" the lips and released a "plague" of words. In every case no matter to whom we were talking or what we said, we made a choice and it could be argued a destructive choice.

The words we speak reveal the person we are, acting as a kind of "microscope" to the heart. If self-exaltation is present in the heart it will be present in speech. If self-absorption is present in the heart it will characterize our talk as well. The lack of self-control "boiling up" in the heart will quickly "boil over" in speech.

The presence of Christ-honoring control in the heart squelches pettiness, defensiveness, retaliation, prideful assertiveness, cold analysis, vain explanation and all else. Godly self-control thwarts the bad before it affects our talk or our walk.

The lesson? When we realize we're about to have an "algae bloom day" we need to keep our mouth turned off more often than not.

Who are the poor assigned to you?

Proverbs 14:21. "He who despises his neighbor sins, but he who has mercy on the poor, happy is he. (NKJ)"

To look down on others is a repugnant form of self-flattery. To conclude that because others have less than us that they ARE less than us uncovers a heart that is less than rich toward God.

We usually hear "mercy" defined as the forgiveness of our sins – of not getting what we deserve. No doubt that defines the main meaning. But in this context "mercy" means something else. It's "giving," not "forgiving." It's taking what's ours and making it theirs.

The church repeatedly and rightly emphasizes giving to the church; our support of ministry is important. But in Scripture we're also commanded to "contribute to the needs of the saints" (Romans 12:13, ESV).

God called Job the most righteous man in the world. In helping the poor, Job was outstanding and worthy of imitation (29:11-16; 31:16-22, ESV): "When the ear heard, it called me blessed, and when the eye saw, it approved, because I delivered the poor who cried for help, and the fatherless who had none to help him. The blessing of him who was about to perish came upon me, and I caused the widow's heart to sing for joy. I put on righteousness, and it clothed me; my justice was like a robe and a turban. I was eyes to the blind and feet to the lame. I was a father to the needy, and I searched out the cause of him whom I did not know."

"If I have withheld anything that the poor desired, or have caused the eyes of the widow to fail, or have eaten my morsel alone, and the fatherless has not eaten of it (for from my youth the fatherless grew up with me as with a father, and from my mother's womb I guided the widow), if I have seen anyone perish for lack of clothing, or the needy without covering, if his body has not blessed me, and if he was not warmed with the fleece of my sheep, if I have raised my hand against the fatherless, because I saw my help in the gate, then let my shoulder blade fall from my shoulder, and let my arm be broken from its socket."

This question remains, who are the "poor" in your life? What are their names? Is it the single mother struggling to make ends meet? Is it the one temporarily out of work? Or is it some other? How much of what you now consider "your" disposable income is better served by giving it out to someone with too little income?

Family "Surround Sound"

Proverbs 15:17. "Better is a dinner of herbs where love is, than a fattened ox and hatred therewith. (ESV)"

This proverb isn't finally about the menu but the diners themselves. Even an affluent family may have:

- more cash than can be safely carried home from the local bank
- the semblance of an uptown traffic jam in the driveway
- every room furnished out to make you want to stay in
- the refrigerator chillin' more food than the local grocery chain
- the TV with access to more cable channels than legs on a centipede

but be as empty of love as an "al Qaeda" counsel meeting.

Just ask those whose family "surround sound" daily amplifies constant criticism and bickering, with frequent verbal jarring and downright meanness, and experiencing repeated nagging and emotional manipulation resulting in constant unrest -- "a fattened ox and hatred with it."

What do you think? At the Last Supper, was Jesus cultivating culinary tastes in bread and wine, or love in His closest disciples? The mutual experience of Christ's character brings a fullness that no meal can touch. And it's certainly much better to enjoy those present at the dinner even more than the dinner itself.

Finally, to enlarge this lesson, we should realize that anytime we gather together in His Name with other Christians, we find ourselves at "His Table"? All those assembled for that "meal" are worth an extraordinary effort: "that you love one another: just as I have loved you, you also are to love one another. (John 13:34, ESV)"

Handling Things by Handing Things Over to the Lord

Proverbs 16:20. "Those who are attentive to a matter will prosper and happy are those who trust in the LORD. (NRS)"

When matters were left in his hands, Paul was beating Christians. When Paul placed all in Christ's hands he was leading Christians, confidently declaring: "for I know whom I have believed, and I am convinced that He is able to guard what I have entrusted to Him until that Day." (2 Timothy 1:12, NAU)

In being "attentive to a matter," what is the one thing applicable to all things? It's the decision to hand it over in trust to the One who is all-wise. We are to rely on His instruction, trust in His abilities and then to act accordingly. "I have had many things in my hands," Martin Luther explained, "and I have lost them all. But whatever I have been able to place in God's hands, I still possess."

What matters then is that we turn over all our matters, great and small, to God and make Him our trust. Happiness begins when our trust in ourselves ends. What's the center verse of the Bible? "It is better to trust in the LORD than to put confidence in man" (Psalm 118:8, KJV). The Christian songwriter, John Sammis, got it right:

Trust and obey, For there's no other way
To be happy in Jesus, Than to trust and obey

Or these words of Jeremiah: "Blessed is the man who trusts in the LORD, whose trust is the LORD," Jeremiah explained. "He is like a tree planted by water that sends out its roots by the stream and does not fear when heat comes for its leaves remain green and is not anxious in the year of drought for it does not cease to bear fruit." (Jeremiah 17:7-8, ESV)

163

Now ask what you have unwisely retained in your own control, operating under the delusion that it's somehow safer in your keeping than in God's? Is it not time to act in accord with this welcome exhortation, "cast your care on Him for He cares for you"?

Avoiding Escalation of Conflict

Proverbs 17:14. "The beginning of strife is like letting out water, so abandon the quarrel before it breaks out. (NAU)"

For two-thirds of my life I've had a dog. Most recently we've had Golden Retrievers. I like dogs. Yet when I was ten years old I encountered Brownie, a definite exception to the "good dog" rule.

One afternoon that mutt jumped up for no good reason and bit me. She'd snapped at other neighborhood kids as well. Brownie definitely needed a semester with The National Geographic Channel's "Dog Whisperer". Don't get me wrong. I didn't stop liking canines that day. But from then on I kept my distance when my neighbor's dog was around.

Relational strife is like Brownie. If you barely provoke it, it may very well jump up and "bite" you. It sometimes comes seemingly out of nowhere, suddenly leaps and nips. This proverb is explicit. Keep an eye on strife. Avoid it. If necessary, go out of your way to walk around it. Don't just venture into Brownie's backyard.

Stop strife at the lowest level possible. Or as the New Testament exhorts: "If it be possible, as much as depends on you, live peaceably with all men." (Romans 12:18, NKJ) Otherwise, you may even develop a reputation like Brownie!

Set your heart today to anticipate the next occasion when strife is about to begin. Determine ahead of time to be the one that abandons the quarrel "before it breaks out" for Christ's sake. And at that moment of opportunity it will pay to recall this blessing:

"May the God of endurance and encouragement grant you to live in such harmony with one another in accord with Christ Jesus that together you may with one voice glorify the God and Father of our Lord Jesus Christ.

Therefore welcome one another as Christ has welcomed you, for the glory of God." (Romans 15:5-7, ESV)

The Only Safe Place in the Universe

Proverbs 18:10. The name of the Lord is a strong tower: the righteous runs into it and is safe. (NAU)"

On that day of days do you recall what was written over His bruised body and bleeding head? Inscribed in Greek, Latin and Hebrew was, "This is Jesus the King of the Jews" (Matthew 27:37; Luke 23:38). THE NAME went international right there at Calvary. The sole entrance then into that strong tower and only safe place in the universe is the cross.

Safe from what then? "Flee the wrath of God," John the Baptist preached. Then introduced the Lord with a hopeful phrase: "Behold! The Lamb of God that takes away the sin of the world!" From every nation and every people-group the elect **run** from divine danger to the Lamb – to the crucified One. "Nor is there salvation in any other: for there is no other name under heaven given among men, by which we must be saved." (Acts 4:12, NKJ)

Safe from what? Regarding earthly dangers, scripture makes it plain that Christians will sometimes experience negatives and evils in the extreme BUT without being separated thereby from Christ: "Who shall separate us from the love of Christ? Shall tribulation, or distress, or persecution, or famine, or nakedness, or danger, or sword? As it is written, `For your sake we are being killed all the day long; we are regarded as sheep to be slaughtered.' No, in all these things we are more than conquerors through him who loved us. For I am sure that neither death nor life, nor angels nor rulers, nor things present nor things to come, nor powers, nor height nor depth, nor anything else in all creation, will be able to separate us from the love of God in Christ Jesus our Lord (Romans 8:35-39, ESV)."

We cannot be too often reminded that our salvation is neither in ourselves nor in this world. It's rather our placement in the "strong tower" that counts. The name of the Lord which we've confessed lifts us up into an unassailable place – to be seated with Christ even in the heavenly places. May the faith of many in these dark days remain secure by safely residing and remaining in the Name of the Lord Jesus Christ.

Developing a Christ-honoring Self-love

Proverbs 19:8. "He who gets wisdom loves his own soul. He who keeps understanding will find good. (NAU)"

"He who loves his life will lose it, and he who hates his life in this world will keep it for eternal life." (John 12:25, NKJ)

Why do those words of Jesus NOT contradict this proverb? As strange as it may sound initially, one way we truly "love" our own soul is to "hate" our life in this world. Christ's intention is not to destroy our soul, but rather to gain something better ("to keep it for eternal life").

Wisdom ever teaches us to deny the inferior for the superior, the lesser for the greater and the temporary for the permanent. Foolishness obscures our ultimate happiness in God by inflating some present competing influence.

Denial resulting in a greater fulfillment is the outcome of Christ's teaching. "He who comes to God must believe that He is and that He is a Rewarder of those who diligently seek Him." (Hebrews 11:6, KJV) C. S. Lewis explains a vital connection between God's wisdom and loving our own soul:

"If you asked twenty good men today what they thought the highest of the virtues, nineteen of them would reply, Unselfishness. But if you asked almost any of the great Christians of old he would have replied, Love. You see what has happened? A negative term has been substituted for a positive. The New Testament has lots to say about self-denial, but not about self-denial as an end in itself. We are told to deny ourselves and to take up our crosses in order that we may follow Christ.

"Nearly every description of what we shall ultimately find if we do so contains an appeal to desire. Indeed, if we consider the unblushing

169

promises of reward and the staggering nature of the rewards promised in the Gospels, it would seem that Our Lord finds our desires not too strong, but too weak." ("The Weight of Glory")

The New Covenant provides an entirely unexpected and revolutionary slant on an acceptable self-love. Ultimately, the wisest way to love our own soul is to love Jesus with all our soul, all our mind, all our heart and all our strength.

Never a man spoke like this Man

Proverbs 20:9. "Who can say, `I have made my heart pure, I am clean from my sin?' (ESV)"

Who can say, "I have made my heart pure, I am clean from my sin"? No one. Who can say, "I have made their hearts clean, I have made them pure from their sin"? Only One – the Lord Jesus Christ.

The fact is that from the time of our conception we are identified by God as sinners. We are by nature "children of wrath." In this deplorable state we are incapable and unwilling of fulfilling what God requires. We cannot offer God what He requires, a perfect life of obedience to His law. Neither can we offer God an acceptable sacrifice to pay for our sins. Thus no one can claim, "I have made my heart pure, I am clean from my sin."

If the truth be known, in our natural state we couldn't care less about God or His law except to disregard both. We are simply worthy, deserving in every way, of abandonment by God and condemnation to death and a bleak future judgment.

If this appears hopeless, that's because it is! And if things only worked on the basis of merit, by earning and deserving, that's how this story would end. But God chose to bring in another covenant headed by His own dear Son. And Jesus saves all those given Him by the Father.

Christ acts on our behalf. He takes down our "old man" through crucifixion and death, fulfilling all the law's demands of perfect obedience, satisfying every judgment against us in the courts of heaven, seeing that we are justified there and also enabling our faith in Him on earth in order to receive all these gracious benefits. The very righteousness and life of Jesus are imputed, credited to them who are His, owing to His grace and received as a free gift.

Who can say, "I have made my heart pure, I am clean from my sin"? No one. Who can say, "I have made their hearts clean, I have made them pure from their sin"? Only One – the Lord Jesus Christ. All credit and praise belong to Him!

Unwanted Voices, Unwanted Needs?

Proverbs 21:13. "Whoever shuts his ear to the cry of the poor will also cry himself and not be answered. (NAU)"

German pastor and survivor of Dachau concentration camp, Martin Niemöller died in 1984 at the ripe old age of 92. Mr. Niemöller was often interviewed about his difficult experience as a minister in Nazi Germany. He was frequently asked how a nation with so much past Christian influence could have succumbed to such a remarkable strain of ungodliness.

In responding to these queries and describing the downward path, Pastor Niemöller surprisingly turned the responsibility on himself: "In Germany they came first for the communists and I didn't speak up because I wasn't a communist. Then they came for the Jews and I didn't speak up because I wasn't a Jew. Then they came for the trade-unionists and I didn't speak up because I wasn't a trade-unionist. Then they came for the Catholics and I didn't speak up because I was a Protestant. Then they came for me and by that time no one was left to speak up."*

The great majority of us will never encounter anything approaching Nazi tyranny. But this proverb describes a much more common occurrence and one that we all do encounter. What do we do with the poor? What do we do with the children of the poor? What do we do with the international poor? What is our involvement? How do we respond typically?

"Whatever we sow, that shall we also reap," the Scripture elsewhere declares. If we are to be heard by God, crying out for our needs to be met, we'd better make the effort to hear and respond to real needs at hand. We'd best deal with our tendency to insulate ourselves from those voices and hiding out behind the blessings and comforts that God graciously allows us to possess!

If we truly hear from God, we'll truly hear the cry of the poor as well. If we become passionate for Christ and His Truth we'll also necessarily become compassionate for people and their needs

Will you ask Jesus Christ today what He would have you to do in setting aside something for someone with legitimate needs and to grant you repeated opportunities to give?

* <u>Christian Century</u>, March 21-28, 1984, p. 296

Wisdom Takes Warning

Proverbs 22:3. "A prudent man sees danger and hides himself, but the simple go on and suffer for it (ESV).**"**

The short-sighted person not only tends to live in the moment but also to live for the moment. That's not a good combination.

In contrast, God's wisdom engenders a faith that listens carefully to counsel even concerning dangers not yet obvious. "By faith Noah, being warned by God concerning events as yet unseen, in reverent fear constructed an ark for the saving of his household. By this he condemned the world and became an heir of the righteousness that comes by faith." (Hebrews 11:7, ESV)

To those who lack this sort of good discretion Jeremiah, the prophet, once exclaimed: "To whom shall I speak and give warning that they may hear? Behold, their ears are closed and they cannot listen. Behold, the word of the LORD has become a reproach to them; they have no delight in it." (Jeremiah 6:10, NAU)

Remember that the Gulf Coast did not take adequate warning with the approach of Hurricane Katrina. Are we responding adequately to clear scriptural warnings? Jesus admonished us to be thoroughly prepared for His return. We've also been informed that we'll appear individually before the Judgment Seat of Christ and there give an account for our lives. Amos preached: "Prepare to meet your God!" The time for adjustment is now!

Arnot commented: "The right place for weighing the worth of any course is on this side of its beginning. Those who rush headlong into a path of conduct because they like it and then begin to consider whether it is a right one will encourage themselves to believe a lie or refuse to follow discovered truth" (*Studies in Proverbs*, p. 130).

We are to live in the moment, fully embracing Christ by enjoying His immense blessings and experiencing His compassionate help in our sufferings. However, we are not to live for the moment. We are to serve the One who is above and beyond all our moments:

"Everyone then who hears these words of mine and does them will be like a wise man who built his house on the rock. And the rain fell, and the floods came, and the winds blew and beat on that house, but it did not fall, because it had been founded on the rock. And everyone who hears these words of mine and does not do them will be like a foolish man who built his house on the sand. And the rain fell, and the floods came, and the winds blew and beat against that house, and it fell, and great was the fall of it." (Matthew 7:24-27, ESV)

Wisdom gives us the ability to identify dangers ahead of time and to comprehend consequences of actions before we make decisions. How is God warning you today?

Wisdom Addresses Heart Matters

Proverbs 23:17-18. "Do not let your heart envy sinners but live in the fear of the LORD always. Surely there is a future and your hope will not be cut off. (NAU)"

Some say the Old Testament was exclusively about obedience to outward standards. And that it's only in the New Testament that we begin to see the ethical stress on inward motives and thoughts. While admitting that the coming of Jesus brought about a much clearer understanding of all things godly, we have to disagree with this too stark OT-NT contrast.

In fact this very proverb shows that the Old Testament was very much concerned with heart attitudes. We should also recall that the 10th commandment, the one forbidding coveting, has everything to do with heart dynamics. As someone observed, coveting is the "mother sin, it gives birth to all the other sins."

Therefore, to read God's commandments <u>properly</u> we must consider the thoughts and motives behind all activity. In the Sermon on the Mount (Matthew 5 especially), Jesus went out of His way to contradict the Pharisees who emphasized obedience to minimal outward aspects of the law.

Thus the Lord indicated that the 7th commandment, the one against adultery, forbids not only the outward act but also <u>all</u> levels of sin leading up to the act. Coveting your neighbor's wife and lust in general are forbidden by this statute. The 6th commandment, the one against murder, forbids the outward act and <u>all</u> levels of sin leading up to the act. That would include wrong anger, provocative words and even demeaning speech.

To "live in the fear of the LORD always" is to be conscious both of the outward and inward dimensions of obedience to Christ. We disobey and disrespect God by envy, whether or not that aspect of covetousness leads to any other transgression.

We must always defer to God's goodness: "surely there is a future and your hope will not be cut off." Faith thinks that and waits with contentment, blessed that God has blessed others.

The Wisdom of Being Magnanimous

Proverbs 24:17. "Do not rejoice when your enemy falls and do not let your heart be glad when he stumbles; or the LORD will see and be displeased and turn His anger away from him. (NAU)"

In Exodus 15, Israel rejoices when their Egyptian enemies perish in the sea. Even Proverbs states approvingly, "when the wicked perish, there is shouting." (11:10)

One seemingly vindictive psalm states: "The righteous will rejoice when he sees the vengeance: he shall wash his feet in the blood of the wicked. So that a man shall say, `Truly there is a reward for the righteous: truly He is a God that judges in the earth.'" (Psalm 58:10-11, NAU) Consult the Book of Joshua and the conquering of Israel's enemies. What of the frequent deliverance God brought during the time of the Judges? or the battles of David – the victories of the mighty men?

When the enemies of Israel fell or died there was rejoicing. So do those incidences of exultation violate the spirit of this proverb? How is it that they do not undermine Christ's teaching to "love our enemies" – to pray for them with good intention – to give back good for evil. (Luke 19:41-44; Matthew 4:44)

It's often necessary to embrace the whole of God's Word in order to clarify a portion of His counsel. This proverb presents yet another instance when there may be more than one godly response; and thus we need the Lord's wisdom to tell us not only "what" to do but "when" to do it.

How do we sort through this "multitude of counsel?" Start on the two sides and then work back towards the middle. When righteousness triumphs and when God brings deliverance, we should rejoice. When imminent dangers from evil are removed, who wouldn't be glad that wickedness didn't win out?

On the other hand it's clear that mere personal vendettas involving revenge certainly fall into a prohibited category. Glorifying God is one thing. Indulging mere personal hatred and vindictiveness is quite another – unlike Jesus Christ.

In sorting through the "Rejoicing" response and the "Not Rejoicing" response, you may be like me. I need more practice in the more difficult lesson. And you can guess which one that is.

Humble Yourself in the
Sight of the Lord

Proverbs 25:6-7. "Do not put yourself forward in the king's presence or stand in the place of the great, for it is better to be told, `Come up here,' than to be put lower in the presence of a noble.' (ESV)"

Harold was fifteen years old at the time. He distinctly remembers walking out of church one Sunday. A group had gathered under a tree a short distance from the building. With curiosity Harold quietly drifted toward the assembly of grown men. The conversation seemed to center on famous people and he was all ears.

One gentleman indicated that he'd met and spent some time with Jackie Robinson in Brooklyn. That sounded impressive! Another volunteered that in his youth he had been friends with Martin King, Jr., in Georgia. Wow, even more impressive! Others discussed their own connections with noted individuals.

Suddenly Harold's grandmother was tugging on his ear and to his horror pulled him aside. He was quite upset and embarrassed: "Why did you do that granny?"

"You're about to find out," she replied.

Once out of earshot this godly lady turned to him, looked him straight in the eyes and stated, "Harold, don't you be hanging around all those men talking about who they think is important and who they don't think is important -- about who they know and who they don't know. I want you to remember this. There's nobody important in the way they're talking but Jesus Himself! Do you hear me?"

Why do we emphasize connections with those we feel are significant and somehow add to our reputation or image? Why do we feel differently about

181

ourselves when around people of a certain status or widely recognized as important? (And somehow "borrowing" from their success and stature?)

The answer is not complicated. We all struggle with pride. When under its seducing spell we all seek associations that will enhance our life in our own opinion and the eyes of others. We covet human recognition for our value and worth.

What did good ole granny discern that day and impart to Harold? Jesus would have us to be the "last of all and the servant of all." Hey, is anyone tugging on your ear today?

Respecting the No Gossip Zone

Proverbs 26.20. "For lack of wood the fire goes out and where there is no whisperer, contention quiets down. (NAU)"

Generally, gossip attempts the impossible feat of raising our own reputation by lowering that of others. "Man is naturally his own grand idol," Leighton wrote. "He would be esteemed and honored by any means. And to magnify that idol self, he kills the name and esteem of others."

In Jeremiah's time gossip had become the raging national past-time: "Beware of your neighbors and put no trust in any of your kin; for all your kin are supplanters and every neighbor goes around like a slanderer." (9:4, NRS) In describing the practice in more modern times William Ellis quipped, "The gossiping sort have a cow's tongue, a smooth side and a rough side."

And as far as what scripture says in reference to behind-the-back-talking-about-others, check this out: "The tongue also is a fire, a world of unrighteousness. The tongue is set among our members, staining the whole body, setting on fire the entire course of life and set on fire by hell." (James 3:6, ESV)

In counter-distinction the New Testament would make "firemen" of us all, skilled at putting out slanders and other enflaming rhetoric:

"Let no unwholesome word proceed from your mouth, but only such a word as is good for edification according the need of the moment, so that it will give grace to those who hear.

"And do not grieve the Holy Spirit of God by whom you were sealed for the day of redemption. Let all bitterness and wrath and anger and clamor and slander put away from you, along with all malice. Be kind to

183

one another, tenderhearted, forgiving one other, as God in Christ forgave you." (Ephesians 4:29-32, ESV)

Will you pre-commit yourself to Christ then that upon the very next occasion offered, you'll resist endorsing or contributing to even what might be remotely called gossip?

Transitioning from Picky Connoisseurs

Proverbs 27:7. "A satisfied soul loathes the honeycomb, but to a hungry soul every bitter thing is sweet. (NKJ)"

Is God pleased with those who are plainly hard to please? There is a great difference between a hungry worshipper and a picky consumer.

Through the years I've noticed that those most mature in the Lord tend to be the most easily pleased. In circumstances, even difficult circumstances, these individuals find the portion that is clearly God's working and emphasize the "sweet" rather than the bitter. They demonstrate a "hungry" soul. Complacency is not their problem.

In relationships, hungry disciples focus on the best in others and do their best to affirm those godly qualities. In listening to preaching and teaching they appreciate content over delivery. Thus they receive from anyone and affirm the value of God's truth whenever and wherever it presents itself. On the other hand, the "satisfied" soul experiences a negative fullness, an "I've-had-enough" outlook. And when it comes to spiritual matters they're demanding connoisseurs. Even the best circumstances produce a degree of dissatisfaction. These discontented individuals have little additional room in their lives for new people. They are so full of themselves that they have no room for anything else.

Jesus recommended this general approach and attitude: "Blessed are those who hunger and thirst for righteousness for they will be filled." We become what we hunger after!

How will you live out this "hunger" in Jesus Christ today? in learning from others, in honoring God through circumstances, in loving people? Will you give up any remaining arrogant "tastes" and designate even the "bitter" as sweet?

What Our Choice of Close Companions Conveys

Proverbs 28:7. "He who keeps the law is a discerning son, but he who is a companion of gluttons humiliates his father. (NAU)"

Everyone's been stopped at a railroad crossing. The lights flash back and forth and the red and white crossbars come down. When the train speeds towards you on the track with the horn blowing, it makes a high-pitched noise. The moment the engine passes however that sound changes and becomes lower in pitch.

What's happening? More sound waves reach your ear as the train approaches but as it moves away you are exposed to fewer waves. In 1842 an Austrian physicist, Christian Doppler, described this phenomenon. It's now known as "The Doppler Effect." Today's weather stations utilize Doppler radar which accurately indicates how fast a storm is approaching for a particular location.

This proverb indicates that our choice of close companions acts as a sort of spiritual "Doppler" radar. Thus selecting friends is invariably a "forecast" involving our underlying values and a lifestyle built around those values. It typically signals our direction and rate of speed regarding godliness as well.

Let's say Jason has selected a majority of close buddies that aren't the least bit interested in pursuing Jesus Christ. What does his choice convey? It shows that he's not planning on following the Lord very closely either – at least at present. As a qualification it could be said that Jason wants to evangelize these individuals. OK, that can certainly be the case. Christians should keep in contact with non-Christians. But where then are Jason's other spiritually-minded companions that do exhibit real commitment to Christ? If there are none or if Jason has abandoned those types of friendships something is definitely amiss!

187

We must keep a keen eye as to when relationships pull us more towards the world and away from Christ. The apostle writes: "Do not be deceived: `Bad company corrupts good morals.'" (1 Corinthians 15:33, ESV)

The appeal in this verse is to the conscience for obedience to God and His law. When conscience and companions collide, as they surely will at some point in life, we must always choose conscience . . . and assert loyalty to God over friendship with the world.

The Redeemer of the Prodigal Son

Proverbs 29:3. "A man who loves wisdom makes his father glad, but he who keeps company with prostitutes wastes his wealth. (NAU)"

This contrast between two sons suggests a well-known parable, the Prodigal Son (Luke 15:11-32). In that story the younger sibling lived out the negative connection first but then turned around. The fallen son got back on track! His restoration and reunion combined to make the father glad.

Sadly, at the very moment of the younger son's repentant return the elder son became a sinking grief to his father. Remember it was the now bitter older brother who divulged the lurid details of his younger sibling's mistakes (v. 29-30).

Jesus is no bitter elder brother! Though he confessed, "I do always those things that please" God, yet the Lord sacrificed His life to *effect* our reconciliation to the Heavenly Father. "While we were still weak, at the right time Christ died for the ungodly. For one will scarcely die for a righteous person - though perhaps for a good person one would dare even to die - but God shows his love for us in that while we were still sinners, Christ died for us. Since, therefore, we have now been justified by his blood, much more shall we be saved by him from the wrath of God. For if while we were enemies we were reconciled to God by the death of his Son, much more, now that we are reconciled, shall we be saved by his life. More than that, we also rejoice in God through our Lord Jesus Christ, through whom we have now received reconciliation. (Romans 5:7-11, ESV)"

Has not Jesus become our wisdom, enabling our return to God? When we love Him, for His spotless character, for His bleeding sacrifice and for His work of grace in making up for our waste, this makes the Heavenly Father extremely glad.

Profiles in Courage

Proverbs 30:29-30. "There are three things which are stately in their march. Even four which are stately when they walk: the lion which is mighty among beasts and does not retreat before any. (NAU)"

The Bible gives us more "Profiles in Courage"* than John F. Kennedy ever did.

To name a few: Moses before a furious Pharaoh, Joshua before a fortified Jericho, Gideon before the forbidding Midianites, David before a formidable Goliath, Elijah before the false prophets, Daniel before famished lions, Esther before the frieze-worthy Persian king, Nehemiah before the fanatical Sanballat, and John the Baptist before a froward Herod. And of course we cannot forget Jesus before all those forceful crowds and before all the fierce earthly rulers.

Throughout history those whom the Lord has strengthened have exhibited boldness, courage, bravery, fearlessness and the like. Standing up, standing true and standing strong, these characteristics come naturally to the lion but supernaturally to Christians. The power of the Holy Spirit turned Peter from cowardly denials to fearless proclamations of Christ. Indeed, "the wicked flee when no one is pursuing but the righteous are bold as a lion." (Proverbs 28:1, NAU)

The problem is that many times we identify only too well with Bert Lahr, the "Cowardly Lion" (of the Wizard of Oz) in search of courage. What will remedy our great deficiency but a bold request to Jesus, asking Him along this line?

"Now, Lord, look upon their threats and grant to your servants to continue to speak your word with all boldness, while you stretch out your hand to heal, and signs and wonders are performed through the name of your holy servant Jesus. And when they had prayed, the place in which they were gathered together was shaken, and they were all filled with the Holy Spirit and continued to speak the word of God with boldness. (Act 4:29-31, ESV)"

In what you're facing today, or in what you're helping another to face, how would Jesus Christ have you to exhibit courage and resolve?

* The book, *Profiles in Courage*, by John F. Kennedy won the Pulitzer Prize in 1957

Author Information

Bill Powell grew up in Newport News, Virginia, and has walked with Christ since 1971. He married Leslie Ford in 1975. They met in 1970 and she was the first person that Bill led to Christ – they have three great sons. Bill attended the University of Richmond (receiving B.A. and M.A. degrees) and became a campus ministry-leader there (1972-1975). He was the founding pastor of Grace Covenant Church in Richmond (1976 through 1996). Bill took an educational sabbatical from 1996 through 1999 and received the M.Div. degree from Reformed Theological Seminary in Charlotte, North Carolina.

Since 2000 Bill has pastored Village Christian Fellowship in Suffolk, Virginia. His enjoyment in teaching and explaining the Scripture and God's ways resulted in writing a daily devotional from the Book of Proverbs. For this book Bill compiled some of these devotionals together for publication.

For more information, consult christourwisdom.com

BUY A SHARE OF THE FUTURE IN YOUR COMMUNITY

These certificates make great holiday, graduation and birthday gifts that can be personalized with the recipient's name. The cost of one S.H.A.R.E. or one square foot is $54.17. The personalized certificate is suitable for framing and will state the number of shares purchased and the amount of each share, as well as the recipient's name. The home that you participate in "building" will last for many years and will continue to grow in value.

THIS CERTIFIES THAT

__YOUR NAME HERE__

HAS INVESTED IN A HOME FOR A DESERVING FAMILY

1985-2005

TWENTY YEARS OF BUILDING FUTURES IN OUR COMMUNITY ONE HOME AT A TIME

1200 SQUARE FOOT HOUSE @ $65,000 = $54.17 PER SQUARE FOOT
This certificate represents a tax deductible donation. It has no cash value.

Here is a sample SHARE certificate:

YES, I WOULD LIKE TO HELP!

I support the work that Habitat for Humanity does and I want to be part of the excitement! As a donor, I will receive periodic updates on your construction activities but, more importantly, I know my gift will help a family in our community realize the dream of homeownership. **I would like to SHARE in your efforts against substandard housing in my community!** *(Please print below)*

PLEASE SEND ME _____ SHARES at $54.17 EACH = $ $_____

In Honor Of: _____

Occasion: (Circle One) HOLIDAY BIRTHDAY ANNIVERSARY

OTHER: _____

Address of Recipient: _____

Gift From: _____ *Donor Address:* _____

Donor Email: _____

I AM ENCLOSING A CHECK FOR $ $_____ PAYABLE TO HABITAT FOR HUMANITY OR PLEASE CHARGE MY VISA OR MASTERCARD *(CIRCLE ONE)*

Card Number _____ Expiration Date: _____

Name as it appears on Credit Card _____ Charge Amount $ _____

Signature _____

Billing Address _____

Telephone # Day _____ Eve _____

PLEASE NOTE: Your contribution is tax-deductible to the fullest extent allowed by law.
Habitat for Humanity • P.O. Box 1443 • Newport News, VA 23601 • 757-596-5553
www.HelpHabitatforHumanity.org